Lincoln's Legacy

Lincoln's Legacy

Ethics and Politics

Edited by
PHILLIP SHAW PALUDAN

University of Illinois Press
URBANA AND CHICAGO

© 2008 by the Board of Trustees
of the University of Illinois
All rights reserved
Manufactured in the United States of America
C 5 4 3 2 1
∞ This book is printed on acid-free paper.

Library of Congress Cataloging-in-Publication Data
Lincoln's legacy : ethics and politics / edited by
Phillip Shaw Paludan.
p.   cm.
Includes bibliographical references and index.
ISBN-13: 978-0-252-03223-3 (cloth : alk. paper)
ISBN-10: 0-252-03223-3 (cloth : alk. paper)
1. Lincoln, Abraham, 1809–1865—Ethics.
2. Lincoln, Abraham, 1809–1865—Political and social views.
3. Lincoln, Abraham, 1809–1865—Influence.
4. United States—Politics and government—1861–1865.
5. Political ethics—United States—Case studies.
6. Presidents—United States—Biography.
I. Paludan, Phillip S., 1938–
E457.2.E842   2008
973.7092—dc22   2007023287

Contents

Introduction

"If you seek his monument, look around you."
—Saying near the tomb of the architect Christopher Wren,
    St. Paul's Cathedral, London.

Abraham Lincoln's legacy is reflected in great and trivial ideas all around the world. Statues of him are found in Russia, China, England, and many other countries. His words are translated into dozens, if not hundreds, of languages. Cities and towns (and laundromats, taco stands, and life insurance companies) are named after him; conferences and celebrations meet throughout the year to repeat and interpret what his life and ideas mean to and for people now. Organizations ranging from the American Civil Liberties Union to the Ku Klux Klan quote him to support their goals. A few authors hate him, but the reaction to their published attacks reveals how seriously both revilers and celebrants take what he said and did.¹ Political speeches echo his name, and politicians try to "get right with Lincoln" in Everett Dirkson's happy phrase.²

What is this legacy, and how do we find it? The essays in this volume identify some lessons from Lincoln's time that seem important to remember. I say that tentatively, not because I doubt Lincoln's importance. His ideas are part of abiding conversation about what human values are and ought to be. He is part of what Daniel Boorstin called the "news that stays news." My caution comes from the difficulty in determining how to apply his ideals in a modern world that is almost a century and a half away from him in time and qualitatively probably beyond him at least a couple of centuries more.

A story is told among historians about a time in the 1960s when the great scholar Don E. Fehrenbacher was lecturing in Boston, which was then in turmoil over school bussing. Inevitably, when time for questions came, someone in the audience asked, "What would Lincoln say about bussing?" Fehrenbacher thought for a moment and then replied, "Lincoln would probably have said, 'What's a bus?'"

Lincoln, however, clearly has something to say about the ideas and issues of our time on a more abstract level. Questions about equality, democracy, the rule of law, leadership in a political and constitutional democracy, and the nation's place in the world, to name a few, can all solicit Lincoln's thinking and perspective, his wisdom in the search for answers.

The four essays that follow discuss how Lincoln thought and acted amid the nation's greatest crisis, a crisis over its stability and survival and over its duties to four million slaves and their children. Applying Lincoln's answers to modern crises and conditions requires thoughtful work, but without him in the conversation modern solutions, modern understanding, would be impoverished.

Three essays in this volume were presented over a three-week period at a conference at the University of Illinois, Springfield in October 2004. My contribution was delivered at the University of Chicago in March of that year at a conference on Lincoln and Democracy.

Mark Summers is the leading scholar of nineteenth-century political corruption. His three major works discuss spoilsmanship in three different eras in that time. His essay places Lincoln in the apparently embarrassing position of party leader operating in a system where victors gained and distributed the spoils of office. One of the most famous spoilsmen was Lincoln's first secretary of war, Simon Cameron of Pennsylvania. When asked about Cameron's ethics, Thaddeus Stevens, one of his rivals, once said, "Well, I don't think he would steal a red hot stove." When the secretary demanded an apology, Stevens replied, "I once said I didn't think Cameron would steal a red hot stove, I take that back."

Rather than deny that Lincoln knew and worked the political mechanisms of his age, Summers describes the interaction between man and system. Presidents consistently must be "politician in chief" as well as commanders. Summers suggests, as no other historian has, the intricacies and imperatives of how executive leadership shaped, and was shaped by, the party system at a time of war.

Mark Neely opens a new vision of Lincoln's relationship to courts in the Civil War period. Neely, in his Pulitzer Prize–winning *The Fate of Liberty* has shown the complexities of civil liberty issues in wartime. He has argued that the number of federal and military arrests for protesting against the war was quite small. Vallandighams and Merrymans were rare birds. Democrats all over the country were free to call Lincoln a dictator, and they did so in often ominous terms. In Wisconsin, Marcus "Brick" Pomeroy hoped that if Lincoln was reelected "we trust some bold hand will pierce his heart with a dagger point for the public good."

Neely turns from platform and editorial pages to courtrooms, where judges with southern sympathies challenged Lincoln's conduct of the war. Previously, historians have argued that the Union judiciary usually "rolled over" during the war. These writers were influenced by a perspective that focused on the Supreme Court. Neely looks at the state level, where he finds judges more than willing to oppose war efforts in the name of the "Constitution." Lincoln thought that assuming the loyalty of men frequently of southern heritage while the Slave Power rebelled was a bad gamble. In civil war, potential enemies were often behind the lines as well as in front of them. The president thought that the Constitution gave him power in times of invasion or rebellion to suspend the privilege of habeas corpus. His judicial adversaries clearly disagreed.

How much beyond the regular forms of due process may a president step? Surely, war and rebellion justify some longer strides but under what individual circumstance? Understanding Lincoln's response to his conflict may enlarge our visions of what modern leaders might or ought not do if their wars differ substantially from that of the 1860s.

William Miller, a philosopher of ethics, brings the question of virtue into discussions of Lincoln's presidency. His challenge is to consider the moral obligations that Lincoln assumed when he placed his hand on a bible and said, "I do solemnly swear that I will faithfully execute the Office of President of the United States, and will to the best of my Ability, preserve, protect, and defend the Constitution of the United States." Lincoln was binding himself not only to protect and preserve the nation but also to do so within the Constitution. Thus he was not free to emancipate the slaves because of his personal prerogative; he had to act under power granted by the Constitution, the war power. He was not free to jail dissidents unless the document authorized suspending the privilege of the writ. Much of Lincoln's alleged slowness to act, explained as canniness or reluctance to act at all, as with Emancipation, takes new meaning when we learn how sacred the oath was to him.

My essay challenges a long-standing truism about Lincoln, that he was the great democrat of the nation's history. That truism survived in a world that found the true Lincoln in a log cabin, emphasized his simplicity, his "salt of the earth" decency, and made him into Everyman. Carl Sandburg invented and helped create that man of the people. I ask for a more careful, perhaps more subtle, analysis. At the foundation of my rendering are several facts. Lincoln wrote only one definition of democracy in his life, he opposed Democrat Andrew Jackson's party throughout his life, he rejected Stephen A. Douglas's "popular sovereignty," and he attacked the racist "herrenvolk democracy" that characterized the party of Jackson.

The modern world resounds with cries that the people must be heard, their will be done. Such rhetoric can too easily be taken as a matter of pride by the anointed ones and their leaders. Because his name carries almost religious authority, Lincoln is often the model for such declarations. Yet I am struck by the fact that what faith he had in people was interwoven with respect for political-constitutional institutions. It is, after all, *"government* of the people ... that shall not perish from the earth." And Lincoln, at a time when he might have been appealing to popular pride, triumphant in victory, instead reminded the nation that it was the "judgments of the Lord" that are "true and righteous altogether." Walking "humbly with thy God" was imperative for a democratic nation. I affirm Lincoln's respect for democratic government but try to make clear how important he thought "government" was in those two words.

Here, then, are four pictures of Lincoln's legacy. I trust they show the abiding importance of Lincoln to this country's, and the world's, conversation about politics, law, and the future of democracy.

1. Lincoln and Democracy

PHILLIP SHAW PALUDAN

> "As I would not be a slave, so I would not be a master. This
> expresses my idea of democracy. Whatever differs from this, to the
> extent of the difference, is no democracy."
> —Abraham Lincoln

The topic "Lincoln and Democracy" on its face appears simple. In part it seems so because of the ubiquitous use of the word *democracy*. We have lived in what we call a democracy for so long, and spoken of ourselves as living in one for so long, that it may be hard to conduct a careful investigation of the concept and its practice. Fish don't usually discover water. But it is important to climb out of the water and see what we have been swimming in, especially now that there is so much talk of bringing democracy to the world. Just what is it we are bringing? Is the democracy we experience exportable? The United States has had nearly four hundred years of popular government in one form or another. Few other places can match that heritage. We need to know what our democracy has been before we start to export it.

First, it is necessary to define and describe terms. At its base, democracy is a government in which the people of a society are the source of its legitimate power and authority. The definition gains an ethical dimension by adding an ancient injunction that democracy is "the lawful rule of the many in the true interests of the community."[1] To some extent, Lincoln was engaged in an effort to add that injunction, as I hope will be clear from what follows. But for now, let's agree that people can exercise and/or express authority in several ways. Democracy can be expressed in a plebiscite—the Napoleon III model. It can also be expressed in participatory democracy, where, as Francesca Poletta says, "Freedom is an endless meeting."[2] There are good democracies and bad ones. The people voted the Ayatollah Khomeni into office, and, famously, the people also chose Adolph Hitler. Ancient Athenians governed whether drunk or sober—and with mixed results. Thucydides, Plato, and Aristotle were not impressed.

Even the U.S. democracy features elements that challenge a belief that "we the people" rule the nation. Leaving aside as quickly as possible the 2000 election, consider Congress. In the U.S. democracy, the people's voice is heard through the representatives they elect. In the House, the people as a nation (as distinguished from a state) speak when they elect the 435 representatives to Congress, but, of course, any individual voice can be and is swamped by other individuals in a district. Even small interest groups can be ignored. According to the 2000 census of Illinois, nineteen members of Congress represent more than twelve million people, one representative for every 632,000 citizens. That is almost as many people as voted for Andrew Jackson nationwide in 1828.

In 1860 the ratio was better than now. There were 243 U.S. representatives who responded to about thirty-one million people, a ratio of about 120,000 people for each representative. As Madison and his cohort intended, the large ratio reduces the impact of any one interest group on a legislator. But that is another way of saying that the voice of the people is likely to be diffused enough as to be almost Delphic (the success of the system may rest in part on it being so). I agree with Edmund Morgan that "the people" is a historical construct, a necessary fiction. There are, of course, people—even perhaps a people—but it is not always clear how the governing process of even the best democratic society we can devise expresses many of their feelings.[3]

Lincoln the Democrat

Surely such ambiguity vanishes where the topic is Lincoln and Democracy. Well, let's not be blinded by familiarity. Of course, public discourse constantly links Abraham Lincoln to democracy. In 1990 Harold Holzer helped Mario Cuomo of New York to produce a collection of Lincoln's writing that would be sold around the world—or at least in Europe and the United States. It was called *Lincoln on Democracy,* and Lincoln has been called the savior of democracy. Another collection of Lincoln's quotations epitomizes the man through the title *Of the People, by the People, for the People.* "Our greatest democrat," Roy Basler called him.[4] He has also been described in images that exude democratic values—a man of the people, whose pithy sayings like "God must have loved the common people he made so many of them" are quoted. His leadership during the Civil War has been described as a "fight for democracy."[5]

Lincoln is so often associated with the word and idea of democracy, however, that few stop to consider what the word might have meant to him or the society he represented. His most remembered words are probably those from the last line of the Gettysburg Address: "We here highly resolve that these dead shall not have died in vain, and that government of the people, by the people and for the people, shall not perish from the earth." Scholars have debated which words he emphasized. Some say he emphasized "*of* the people, *by* the people." Others say he emphasized "the *people*."[6] It is also possible that he emphasized "*that government*" to give his words a specific focus on the United States. I happen to think that Lincoln emphasized "*government*" and will suggest why in the rest of this essay.

It is certainly the case that he believed in a government of and for the people. He also believed that as a legislator he should be guided by the will of his constituents when he knew what that will was. That contrasted with some members of his Whig Party who maintained they had been elected for their personal judgment, and thus there were times when a lawmaker did what he thought right even if his district seemed opposed.[7] Lincoln was no fool; he spoke of the people on many occasions. His rise from very humble origins proved that anyone's son could be elected president. It is not wrong to call Lincoln a believer in democratic government.

But that designation needs refinement. He did not assume the goodness of the public will. It would be very surprising had he said what Andrew Jackson did: "Never for a moment believe that the great body of the citizens . . . can deliberately intend to do wrong."[8] Pure Jacksonian democracy frightened Lincoln for it seemed to nurture the instability of most idealized abstractions. His faith in democracy was not abstract or ideal; it focused on the processes of American democracy. It focused on how democracy worked, not what it claimed to be. Above all, it rested on his devotion to the restraints of order, law, the Constitution, and history.

The search for order was the foundation of Lincoln's personality. When Lincoln was a teenager, his good friend Matthew Gentry went insane before his eyes. The experience so haunted Lincoln that as late as 1846, twenty-one years thereafter, he wrote a poem about his memories of childhood. The work contains twenty-four stanzas, half of which are about Gentry's madness.[9]

Self-control meant also mastering his future by escaping from the often chaotic, backward, and poorly educated world of subsistence farming. After trying work as a shopkeeper, he taught himself to be a surveyor and learned the mathematics required for that job. Then he turned to the law and mastered the skill in logic that profession demands. Lincoln worked as a lawyer for more than a quarter of his life—nothing else he did absorbed so much of his existence. Whatever his skills in persuading juries through bonhomie and emotional appeal, and they were formidable, Lincoln made a career in law because he had a powerful mind and considerable knowledge of the rules and rationalizations of the discipline. That knowledge and skill translated into the political realm when he began debating Stephen A. Douglas and gained success there by his logic as well as passion. Lincoln, despite protesting that he would not be a master, had in fact become the master of his circumstances and much of his fate.

In short, Lincoln spoke to the mind, believed in the power of reason, and feared that simple appeals to public passions could be demagoguery. He believed that the mind should control the heart and spoke to what he saw as the better angels of our nature by appeals to reason.

Theories of democracy fit only tangentially into this worldview. Lincoln was not particularly interested in the concept of democracy. He didn't spend much time thinking or speaking directly about it.[10] According to the eight volumes of the *Collected Works,* he used the word *democracy* 138 times and provided only one definition of what he meant: "As I would not be a slave, so would I not be a master. This expresses my idea of democracy. Whatever differs from this, to the extent of the difference is no democracy." The statement is a fragment that Lincoln wrote on a sheet of paper but sent to no one; it appears nowhere else in his speeches or writing. We have it because Mary Lincoln gave it to Myra Bradwell in gratitude for helping free Mary from the asylum. Given the available records, it seems safe to say that Lincoln did not clearly define democracy for any assemblage of Americans in his lifetime, perhaps not even for himself.

Something might also be gained by noting the frequency and timing of the word. All but eighteen of Lincoln's usages of the word *democracy* came before he was president. According to volumes 5 and 6 of the *Collected Works,* which cover the period from October 1861 to October 1863, he did not use the word at all; volume 7 records him using it once. In the last years of his life, covered by volume 8 (September 12, 1864 to April 14, 1865), he did not use the word, and from October 1861 to his death Lincoln used "democracy" one time, according to the information we have. By contrast, he used words reflecting order much more; "law" is used 1,323 times and "constitution" 1,437. That totals 2,760 instances of usage, or twenty times more than "democracy" (138).

Of course, 138 times constitute quite a few uses of a word. In almost every case, however, Lincoln almost always referred to the Democratic Party, which its supporters called the "Democracy." He seldom had much good to say about it, whether the herrenvolk democracy of Andrew Jackson, the Manifest Destiny democracy of James K. Polk, or the popular sovereignty democracy of Stephen Douglas.

In fact, Lincoln had an ongoing quarrel with democracy, a lover's quarrel no doubt but a quarrel nonetheless. I'm inclined to think that I could entitle a book *Lincoln's Quarrels with Democracy*. The story would rest on examples like the following: In his famous Lyceum Address in January 1838, Lincoln spoke about democracy's dangers. He was responding to recent events when mobs had attacked bank directors in Baltimore, hanged a gambler on the Mississippi, killed Elijah Lovejoy for printing an abolitionist newspaper, murdered blacks in Mississippi, and burned a black man to death in St. Louis. Lincoln also spoke at a time when Whigs were attacking Democrats as demagogues and their leader, Jackson, as a "concentrated mob." Lincoln was certainly a Whig in his concerns about what Jacksonianism was spawning.[11]

As a cure for all this disorder Lincoln offered no explanation or justification of popular will. Instead, he demanded that reverence for the law become the "political religion of the nation. . . . [L]et every lover of liberty, every well wisher to his posterity, swear by the blood of the revolution never to violate in the least particular the laws of the country, and never to tolerate their violation by others. . . . Let reverence for the laws, be breathed by every American mother to the lisping babe that prattles on her lap. . . . Reason, cold, calculating unimpassioned reason, must furnish all the materials for our future support and defense."[12]

He repeated himself four years later when he spoke to the local Temperance Society in Springfield. Ending his address favoring temperance, Lincoln connected intemperance with the unleashing of fatal passions and called for those passions to be defeated, as he put it, in "the happy day when, all appetites controlled, all passions subdued, all matters subjected, mind, all conquering mind, shall live and move the monarch of the world. Glorious consummation! Hail fall of Fury! Reign of Reason, all hail."[13]

Lincoln therefore respected ordered reason and feared a democratic society in which the mind failed to restrain passions. It is not altogether surprising that he opposed outbreaks of democracy in many of its forms. Jacksonian mobs found echo in Douglas's popular sovereignty, where citizens on the spot determined slavery's fate. Senator Douglas rested his argument for popular sovereignty on the abiding democratic principle that popular majorities had the right to enact their will. The debates with Douglas were essentially about popular sovereignty—the right of local governments to make their own laws for their safety and prosperity. But Lincoln placed equality ahead of democracy. Douglas argued that the people of a territory, voting by majority votes, could include or exclude slavery from that territory. Local democracy should speak authoritatively in the territories, but Lincoln insisted that Congress had control over the territories and could therefore trump majority will there. One could say that Lincoln's appeal to congressional authority might reflect his embrace of the "government of the people" or perhaps of "We the People" over a localistic, state's (or territorial) rights claim. Clearly, however, democracy as experienced in the territories was closer to the voice of the people there than was the outreach of Congress. It was less moral but more democratic.

Lincoln brought in the heavy artillery to attack popular sovereignty in the territories. The Kansas-Nebraska Act was morally wrong and also unleashed disorder. It was "conceived, in violence, passed in violence . . . maintained in violence and . . . executed in violence." He challenged secession, surely a democratic movement in Dixie, as the "essence of anarchy." Lincoln hesitated very little in limiting the people's voice. He limited, and at times stifled, speech and the press during the conflict. His efforts were hardly enough to make him a dictator but sufficient to make civil liberties a major campaign issue for the Democratic Party. The chilling of popular discussion ought to make us wonder at the extent to which he was the voice of unqualified democracy in both senses.[14]

Other aspects of Lincoln's thinking raise doubts about his alleged commitment to democracy. According to a famous adage, you can fool all the people some of the time and some of the people all the time but you can't fool all the people all the time.[15] No one has found evidence that Lincoln said those words, but many people attribute them to him, assuming that something about the phrase seems to fit.[16] What, then, was Lincoln saying about most of the people—that they are fooled most of the time?

Of course, there are other words that define democracy. What about "people"? Lincoln is linked with "the people" because of the Gettysburg coda. He is recorded as using "the people" 1,282 times in the eight-volume collection: 182 times in volume 1, 244 times in volume 2, 493 times in volume 3, 161 times in volume 4, seventy-five times in volume 5, thirty-nine times in volume 6, forty-five times in volume 7, and forty-three times in volume 8. The more he matured, the less Lincoln found uses for the phrase. It seems possible that Lincoln was a man of the people, that he governed for the people, but that he seems not to have been committed to a government by the people. His major commitment was to a government that governed the people and to the equality on which democracy rested rather than to democracy and/or "the people" themselves.

Yet for all the questions about Lincoln's links to democracy in the public domain, he seems to have been personally a democrat in treating people as though he recognized that they were equal with himself, especially African Americans such as Sojourner Truth and Frederick Douglass. "Here comes my friend, Douglass," Lincoln shouted at the 1865 inaugural reception, and the president had well-publicized meetings with the former slave and other black men. Truth recalled that "I never was treated by anyone with more cordiality and warmth, I felt that I was in the presence of a friend." Lincoln also met in the White House with large numbers of ordinary people. As William E. Seward observed, "[T]here was never a man so accessible to all sorts of proper and improper persons."[17]

Lincoln's personal democratic instincts can be seen also in his attitudes about racial equality. Most of the more recent scholarship on Lincoln has focused on his belief, or lack thereof, in equality. Lerone Bennett, editor of *Ebony* magazine, energized this debate in a five-hundred-page book in which he insisted that Lincoln was a racist. Many scholars, myself included, have demonstrated the flaws in that argument. The debate about "Lincoln: Honky vs. Egalitarian" does, however, provide insights into the question of Lincoln's democracy. Democracy rests on the idea of equality. A government of the people and by the people is one without a natural or established hierarchy. Governments by popular consent rest on the idea that all who are governed have an equal right to be heard about how that will be accomplished. That is the theory of the Declaration of Independence. Because of the self-evident truth that all men are created equal we established our government on the consent of the governed.[18]

Lerone Bennett notwithstanding, Lincoln's commitment to equality was strong, and it grew as he aged and became president. Early comments about not wanting blacks to vote or serve on juries were forgotten as black soldiers and sailors proved their courage and discipline. During his presidency Lincoln emancipated more than two million slaves, initiated the Thirteenth Amendment ending slavery throughout the United States, and recruited and used blacks in the military. He advocated black voting and probably was on the way to protecting civil rights for blacks in Dixie.

Despite these public acts, more recent authors have denied that Lincoln was personally an egalitarian. It is true that he told racist jokes and enjoyed minstrel shows, yet the jokes in Paul Zall's *Abe Lincoln Laughing* are mild ones. Did Lincoln like minstrel shows? Yes. But according to *Lincoln Day by Day* he only attended two of them in his entire life. His commitment to equality is well established and secure, but his egalitarian instincts cannot be confused with faith in pure democracy. He understood the equation, the connection, between equality and democracy. His commitment to equality was in a legal sense, however, not in a belief that all men behaved with equal probity and the pure-of-heart democrat deserved trust because, theoretically, he was equal to all other people. For Lincoln, equality was a proposition rather than a goal achieved. So was democracy.[19]

The Presidency and Democracy

When Lincoln came to the presidency he walked into a crisis of law and order. The newspapers and speeches of the time all mention "enforcing the law," stopping disorder, and assert that successful secession would loose the bonds of order and produce successive secessions. For Lincoln, that meant "anarchy."[20]

To preserve that order Lincoln willingly limited democracy. He denied the right of the people of Dixie to exercise the consent of the governed to rebel against a government that in their eyes threatened their rights. Elected by fewer than 40 percent of the popular vote, he suspended the privilege of the writ of habeas corpus without awaiting congressional consent. He accepted Secretary of State Seward's and then War Secretary Edwin M. Stanton's crackdowns on freedom of the press by censoring and closing some newspapers. He countenanced the arrest of Clement Vallandigham for making a speech challenging Gen. Ambrose E. Burnside's order against "disloyal" speech and employed an ominous justification for doing so: "The man who stands by silently while the fate of his country is being discussed cannot be misunderstood. If not stopped he is sure to help the enemy."[21]

Mark Neely has shown that most of the "arbitrary arrests" of the time were made as the Union Army advanced into rebel territory—few of those made by Lincoln stifled political dissent. Large numbers of Democrats, however, used and followed Roger Taney's argument in *ex parte Merryman* that Lincoln was the enemy, not the supporter, of democratic speech. It is certainly true that racism was a powerful card in the Democrats' arsenal, but attacks on Lincoln's civil liberty actions were of substantial power as well. Otherwise, why would Democrats have continued to use the accusation in their newspapers and from platforms throughout the conflict? It is also true that Lincoln supported restricting the press. Although the majority of newspapers stayed open and called him a tyrant, it was enough to make an example of a few to instruct others on the limits of dissent. Lincoln did not act directly but he allowed Seward and Stanton to pursue their arrests and closures.[22]

Yet another side of Lincoln's presidency nurtured and enlivened democracy. In simplest terms, he expanded the processes of democracy in two major ways. First, he began the process of expanding the electorate to include African Americans. Emancipation was his first step, and he also encouraged states to let "very intelligent" blacks and those who were veterans vote. In his last major speech he told the nation that was his wish. National voting rights were five years in the future, but without these early steps no promises could be made.[23] Furthermore, he had laid the groundwork for black voting by enlisting African Americans as soldiers.

Second, in saving the Union Lincoln had played a major role in the two major prizes of the conflict, both foundational to the nation's democratic government. With the Union secure from successful secession, no state could ever again defy the peaceful ways established by the Constitution and change the government. As Lincoln told a Republican colleague before war began:

> We have just carried an election on principles fairly stated to the people. Now we are told in advance, the government shall be broken up, unless we sur-render to those we have beaten, before we take the offices. In this they are either attempting to play upon us, or they are in dead earnest. Either way, if we surrender, it is the end of us, and of the government. They will repeat the experiment upon us *ad libitum*. A year will not pass, till we shall have to take Cuba as a condition upon which they will stay in the Union. They now have the Constitution, under which we have lived over seventy years, and acts of Congress of their own framing, with no prospect of their being changed; and they can never have a more shallow pretext for breaking up the government, or extorting a compromise, than now.[24]

With slavery destroyed, the fundamental cause of such defiance was gone. The leading source of attacks on civil liberties for whites and blacks was also destroyed. People now were free to attack racism and bondage with-out being mobbed, at least in the North and for a time in the South. They could print challenges to servitude without presses being destroyed or editors murdered. Lawmakers could speak on the floor of Congress without fear of brutal beatings. The imperative open discourse of the polity was words, not physical violence. Killing slavery unleashed the arguments and conversations on which democratic government lived. Lincoln helped emancipate more than slaves.

The Ongoing Vitality of the Democratic Process

In a larger sense, war gave vitality to the electoral process. No northern state, city, or county missed a single election in the four years of fighting. There was a presidential election of 1864. People could see and, reflected in every ballot, touch the government they were fighting to preserve.[25] Keeping the war going, as Lincoln did, allowed Americans to experience the vitality of their polity in the face of crisis. They found it did very well. Throughout the war even soldiers remained political partisans—"thinking bayonets." Campfire discussion was frequently political, pitting Democrats against Republicans. Soldiers were furloughed to go home and vote because they wanted to exer-cise their franchise as well as to see loved ones; those who cast their ballots in 1864 did so for the man who promised more war. Those who voted for

George B. McClellan were not unknown in the army; overall, Democratic totals were substantial. More votes were cast in the free states for McClellan than for Douglas and John C. Breckenridge combined four years before.[26] Despite the disruptions of war, an estimated 78 percent of eligible voters went to the polls, closely approximating the 81 percent who voted in 1860. All this demonstrated the vigor of the self-governing process. As one observer noted just after the wartime election of 1864, "The bubble of Republicanism, which was to display such alacrity at bursting, is not the childish thing it was once deemed. . . . We have proved that we are a nation equal to the task of self-discipline and self control."[27]

If Lincoln privileged government and law above democracy he still had some faith in the people, but it was a faith that ebbed and flowed. He told Congress in July 1861 that "the people will save their government, if the government itself, will do its part, only indifferently well." And when he described loyalty in the early days he noted that although officers in the military had deserted, no enlisted man had done so.[28] The people were patriotic, and Lincoln admired that. As the war went on, however, and defeats and victories alternated he often worried about the depth of that patriotism.

Throughout the conflict, whenever Union forces met a defeat Lincoln wondered anxiously, "What will the people think?" In fact, the people may have been better than Lincoln thought, for they endured four years of conflict and the bloodiest war in the nation's history. They kept on sending their sons to battle, and thousands reenlisted. Hundreds of thousands bought bonds, paid taxes, and voters kept on sending war advocates to Congress. Lincoln still wondered, however, how good the people might be.

In 1864 he had a conversation with John Hay that may suggest where Lincoln stood on democracy. They were discussing the Democrat convention of 1864 when Lincoln expressed the opinion that leading politicians would try and push the gathering "to some violent end, but they cannot transfer the people, the honest though misguided masses to the same course." Hay disagreed. He thought the "barefooted Democracy from the heads of the hollows who are now clearly for peace would carry everything in the Convention before them."[29] The people needed guidance. Untutored democracy exuded honesty but required instruction; war and the president who led it provided that instruction.

Lincoln was serious about his bully pulpit. He was the nation's propagandist (persuader)-in-chief. He molded public opinion and provided the guidance that people needed. He carefully watched to see that his speeches were reported correctly. He justified his wartime actions with public letters defending the supplying of Fort Sumter, the so-called arbitrary arrests, the draft, and his reconstruction policy. He encouraged the widespread pamphleteering by the Union League, the Loyal Publication Society. All these were natural and abiding parts of the president's job, but they illustrate how much Lincoln thought the people needed teaching and guidance.[30]

It seems that Lincoln did not believe the people were ignorant. They were fickle, but they were capable of understanding. They could rise above their passions and employ reason to find their paths. Lincoln eschewed appeals to the hatreds and the fears of his audiences. He never referred to the Confederacy or its people as evil. He treated political opponents as rational men who had constituencies to represent, not personal enemies. Politics was not personal for Lincoln. He appealed to the better angels of the people's nature, showing them that he respected their capacity to reason and bear malice toward none. In treating the people in that way, he showed that he respected them.[31]

That respect, perhaps a core idea, is best revealed in an area where the nature of Lincoln's democratic ideals is evident: the Second Inaugural address. In the greatest of his speeches, Lincoln never once mentioned the people, nor democracy, nor the triumph of a free people's government over its enemies. What he did focus upon is a worldview, a frame of mind and heart that is probably fundamental to any successful democracy. It is encompassed in a verse from the Bible: "O man what is good and what doth the lord require of thee, but to do justly, and to love mercy, and to walk humbly with thy God?" (Micah 6:8). Lincoln had always questioned the notion that God gave clear commands to the righteous. His Temperance Address spoke of the need for human reason and humility to inspire reform efforts. When people came to the White House to tell him what God wanted him to do, he would joke a bit by wondering aloud why God would be talking to others about his job and not directly to him. When reminded that God was on America's side, Lincoln replied that he hoped to put America on God's side. The country was perhaps "an almost chosen people," but it seemed arrogance to say that God wore blue or red, white, and blue.[32]

And Lincoln epitomized that view in the Second Inaugural. It was a time of triumph, and throughout the North people celebrated, exulted, and spoke of the victory of their ideas and how that victory showed that God endorsed their ideals. Lincoln, however, warned about avoiding pride and triumphalism and urged people to recognize that God's purposes transcend human understanding. His message surprised its audience for that reason.[33] It was an admonition to people of the victorious North not to take too much pride in themselves. Unlike Jackson's ringing endorsement of popular will ("never for a moment believe that the great body of the citizens . . . can deliberately intend to do wrong"), Lincoln instilled doubt rather than arrogance.[34] His comments on humility and respect for higher authority provided an opposing voice to democratic arrogance, an admonition to humility, and doubt about being self-righteous. They reminded the nation that God might administer discipline, punishing those responsible for the sin of slavery, and the president included both North and South in the indictment.

The Democracy of Lincoln's day was associated with deep racism, arrogant manifest destiny, and pervasive self-glorification of the nation, all of which made foreign visitors wince. As the war wound down, however, the Union Army had proven itself to be powerful and inexorable in gaining victory. People easily believed that righteousness as they understood it (and even knew it) should prevail. Lincoln, however, asked for humility, doubt, and recognition that "the Almighty has His purposes." It was a warning to a people, a democracy, that he believed needed the instruction and humble guidance of its leaders and of God as "God gives us to see the right." What is at issue is whether that warning has been understood or can be relevant.[35] Maybe Lincoln's humility is the most significant thing to recall about his American democracy. Democracy without the rule of law and reason, lacking a sense of self-doubt, may not be what is needed in years to come.

2. The Exacting Legacy of a Virtuous President

WILLIAM LEE MILLER

At noon on March 4, 1861, the moral situation of Abraham Lincoln of Illinois was abruptly transformed. That morning, arising in the Willard Hotel at Fourteenth Street and Pennsylvania Avenue in downtown Washington, he had been a private citizen, an individual moral agent. That afternoon, standing on the steps of the East Portico of the Capitol before thirty thousand fellow citizens, he had become an oath-bound head of state. Constitutional wizardry had transmuted him into the "executive" of the federal government of the United States, the position the Framers in Philadelphia seventy-four years before had decided to call by the word *president*. There abruptly settled upon his elongated frame a profound new responsibility that obligated, constrained, and empowered him. He would transform the office—and the office would transform him.

A First Virtue: The Oath to Preserve the Nation

For Lincoln, taking the oath had a depth and a breadth of moral meaning that went beyond what the act had meant for his immediate predecessors. For him, it was a personal and categorical moral commitment to preserve a nation whose integrity was uniquely in peril.

He had focused on the oath from the time he became aware that he would become president. Back in January of 1861 in Springfield he hid away in a dingy, dusty back room upstairs over a store to compose his inaugural address, and he started and ended with the oath. South Carolina had already passed its ordinance of secession and celebrated with fireworks on December 20. Six other Deep South states followed. Although they claimed to have seceded, Lincoln, in a kind of secret counterpoint, was writing that what they were doing was "legally nothing" (William E. Seward in Washington would persuade him to change "nothing" to the lawyer's word *void*).[1]

He began his address by saying, "In compliance with a custom as old as the government itself, I appear before you to address you briefly, and to take, in your presence, the oath prescribed by the Constitution of the United States, to be taken by the President 'before he enters on the execution of his office.'"[2]

When he came to the end of the speech as he first wrote it in Springfield, he sharply distinguished his moral situation from that of the rebels: "In your hands, my dissatisfied fellow countrymen, and not in mine, is the momentous issue of civil war." He explained that radical moral difference by reference to his oath: "*You* have no oath registered in Heaven to destroy the government, while *I* shall have the most solemn one to "preserve, protect, and defend" it. *You* can forbear the *assault* upon it; *I* can not shrink from the defense of it." What he was saying was that the "dissatisfied countrymen"—the rebels, whom he was addressing—were still in the moral realm of calculation and possibility, but he would be in the different moral realm of imperative and necessity. He would have a sworn oath, a solemn self-binding promise; they would not. They could act differently; he could not. For him, the moral claim would be categorical; for them it was hypothetical; for him, imperative, for them, discretionary. He would take a most solemn oath—they would have no such oath. The oath would be "registered in heaven"; they had no such heavenly registration for any purpose. He could not shrink; they were not prevented from altering their course of action. He planned to finish in the last words he would speak, echoing out across the inaugural day crowd and across the nation: "With you, and not with me, is the solemn question of 'Shall it be peace, or a sword?'"[3]

When he got to Washington he changed that ending. He took Seward's suggestion that there be a more conciliatory ending, and, showing literary and rhetorical power of a new sort and working in the Willard Hotel under the intense pressures of the last week, he converted Seward's raw materials by the alchemy of his editing from dross into gold.

Before Lincoln would come to the mystic chords of memory and better angels of our nature at the end of the address as he would finally give it, there was still in the penultimate paragraph a sharp distinction between his moral situation and that of his dissatisfied countrymen: "You have no oath registered in Heaven to destroy the government, while I shall have the most solemn one to 'preserve, protect, and defend' it."

Sitting behind him on the platform was another man who had taken that presidential oath, James Buchanan, with whom Lincoln had ridden down

Pennsylvania Avenue past the crowds, the riflemen watching from rooftops. Buchanan had a different view of the meaning of the oath. He had not felt any presidential duty, nor found any constitutional power, to resist the secession of South Carolina on the previous December 20 or of six other states in the following months. In December, after Lincoln's election, Buchanan had sent Congress a weirdly self-contradictory annual message full of astonishing reversals that ended nowhere. He blamed the crisis entirely on "the incessant and violent agitation of the slavery question throughout the North for the last quarter of a century." That agitation, Buchanan said, "Has at length produced its malign influence on the slaves and inspired them with vague notions of freedom." This American president deplored this section of the human family being inspired by "vague notions of freedom" not because of vagueness but because of freedom.

President Buchanan had described the result in language that might have come from a secessionist firebrand: "Hence a sense of security no longer exists around the family altar. This feeling of peace at home has given place to apprehensions of servile insurrections. Many a matron throughout the South retires at night in dread of what may befall herself and children before the morning." Then, having accepted and given voice to his southern friends' diagnosis, he astonished everyone by rejecting their prescription. He denied any constitutional right to secede. He insisted, as Lincoln would, that the Union is perpetual. There were sentences in this part of his message that Lincoln could have taken into his inaugural address. Buchanan said, for example, that to regard the Union as a mere voluntary association of states would make it a "rope of sand" (a figure of speech Lincoln could have used), with the thirty-three states becoming "as many petty, jarring, and hostile republics," a dramatization of a point Lincoln would make and James Madison had made.[4]

But at that point, having astonished many who did not think the weak and vacillating Buchanan (as they had come to think of him) had the fortitude to oppose secession, he reversed the astonishment by arguing that if, nevertheless, a state did resist, did secede, there was nothing the federal government could do about it. It could not "coerce" a state. There was, more specifically, nothing a president could do about a state seceding.

Buchanan was inclined to belittle the president's role as "a mere executive officer." "He is no more than the Chief Executive officer of the government. His province is not to make but to execute the laws. . . . The Executive has no authority to decide what shall be the relations between the federal government and South Carolina," said Buchanan.[5]

William Seward, about to become Lincoln's secretary of state, had given a witty summary of President Buchanan's message: "It shows conclusively that it is the duty of the President to execute the laws—unless somebody opposes him; and that no state has the right to go out of the Union—unless it wants to."[6]

That would not be Lincoln's view. Where Buchanan sought avoidance and found restriction and therefore excuse, the new president would accept responsibility and find necessity and therefore empowerment. Whereas President Buchanan had not believed that that oath required him to resist secession, or that the Constitution permitted him to, Lincoln believed that the Constitution did permit him to resist and that his oath required him to.

The chief justice who administered that oath certainly did not think it required, or the Constitution permitted, any such thing. When Lincoln, on Inauguration Day, finished delivering his address there arose on the platform a withered, aged, and stooped figure, a "gnarled corpse" who came forward accompanied by a clerk holding a large bible. This was Roger Taney, author of the *Dred Scott* decision and now about to serve as chief justice under his ninth president. The chief justice inaudibly administered the oath, the clerk holding the bible, and the new president spoke the most solemn oath, registered, as he put it, in heaven. The two men radically disagreed over what it meant: "I, Abraham Lincoln, do solemnly swear that I will faithfully execute the Office of President of the United States, and will to the best of my Ability, preserve, protect and defend the Constitution of the United States."

Before three months would pass Lincoln would have occasion to make a striking reference to his oath in an exchange with the chief justice. Taney, altogether sympathetic to slavery and secession, challenged the new president's suspension of the writ of habeas corpus in Maryland as that state teetered on the brink of secession. He turned a constitutional phrase into a challenge to Lincoln. One who has sworn to "take care that the laws be faithfully executed," said the chief justice, should not himself violate those laws.[7]

Lincoln made a famous response in his message to the Special Session: "[A]re all the laws, *but one,* to go unexecuted, and the government itself go to pieces, lest that one be violated? . . . would not the official oath be broken, if the government should be overthrown, when it was believed that disregarding the single law, would tend to preserve it?"[8] The distinguished twentieth-century constitutional lawyer Edward Corwin would write that this reference to the oath is the "outstanding precedent . . . for treating the oath as a source of power" and that Lincoln permanently recruited power for the presidency, recruited it, that is, from the presidential oath."[9]

But is it not a rather curious foreshortening of the meaning of an oath to treat it as a "source of power"? Is not the word *recruit* a rather odd choice of verb in this connection? "On its face," as lawyers say, an oath is not a distribution of power but a moral commitment, heightened promise, and solemn engagement of the self set in some frame of ultimate obligation. If there is any "recruiting," then it is the moral agent being recruited, and seriously engaged, to conduct himself in a specified way.

Surely one should deal with an oath in the realm of the rights and wrongs of human conduct before inquiring what that might mean in the realm of power. As Lincoln would write in 1864, "Nor was it my view that I might take an oath to get power, and break the oath in using the power."[10] The oath was a moral definition and limitation of his conduct. Others would point to the immense *power* that in that moment came into his hands. He would point instead to the constraining *duty* that was antecedent to and the reason for the power.

He wrote the draft of the "all the laws but one" passage in the message to the Special Session in the first person so the requirements that the oath placed upon him personally, as a responsible moral agent, were more forcefully expressed. He wrote, "I should consider my official oath broken, if I should allow the government to be overthrown, when I might think the disregarding of a single law would tend to preserve it."[11]

A Second Virtue: Rhetorical Power

Before Lincoln took the oath he gave a clearly argued inaugural address. He showed again, as he had done a year before at Cooper's Union and in the six years before that, his ability to write excellent speeches.

Of course, he did the writing himself. And, of course, he did the thinking himself. If we were to make a full list of this president's virtues, his ability to articulate the nation's ideals would rank very high. He did so not only in the two great short productions of his presidency that would attain worldwide fame but also in two important productions of 1861 in which he made the fundamental argument: his inaugural address and his message to the Special Session of July 4.

As the distinguished literary critic Edmund Wilson would write, "Alone among American Presidents, it is possible to imagine Lincoln, grown up in a different milieu, becoming a distinguished writer of a not merely political kind."[12] Defenders of other presidential scribblers may cite Theodore Roosevelt and Woodrow Wilson, who certainly produced books, which Lincoln never did, and above all Thomas Jefferson, whose talent with the pen led John Adams to yield the drafting of the Declaration to the younger man. But Wilson no doubt meant by the phrase "of a not merely political kind" to claim for Lincoln the possibility of a distinctly literary excellence beyond merely serviceable political prose.

Wilson wrote of "the tautness and the hard distinction that when, disregarding legends, we attack Lincoln's writings in bulk." In the public utterances and the official correspondence of the presidency, Wilson wrote, one finds "a Lincoln intent, self-controlled, strong in intellect, tenacious of purpose. . . . His own style was cunning in its cadences, exact in its choice of words, and yet also instinctive and natural; and it was inseparable from his personality in all of its manifestations. This style pervades Lincoln's speeches, his messages to Congress, his correspondence with his generals in the field as well as with his friends and family, his interviews with visitors to the White House and his casual conversation."[13]

In his youthful efforts there had been a certain amount of purple prose, of rodomontade, but Lincoln, by the time he became president, "is working for the balance of eighteenth-century rhythms, and he learns to disembarrass these of eighteenth-century pomposity. He will discard the old-fashioned ornaments of forensic and congressional oratory, but he will always be able to summon an art of incantation with words, and he will know how to practice it magnificently—as in the farewell address to Springfield, the Gettysburg speech and the Second Inaugural Address—when a special occasion demands it."[14]

As to the comparison with Jefferson, there is a passage in Carl Becker's *The Declaration of Independence* on something missing in Jefferson's style that can be found in Lincoln's. Becker compares a tortured piece of the rejected passage on slavery from the draft of the Declaration with the great penultimate passage in Lincoln's Second Inaugural that begins, "Fondly do we hope—fervently do we pray—that this mighty scourge of war may speedily pass away," and ends, "[T]he judgments of the Lord are true and righteous altogether." Of that passage Becker observes, "There is a quality of deep feeling . . . an indefinable something which is profoundly moving; and this something, which informs and enriches much of Lincoln's writing, is rarely, almost never, present in the writing of Jefferson. . . . This something, which Jefferson lacked but which Lincoln possessed in full measure, may perhaps for want of a better term be called a profoundly emotional apprehension of experience."[15]

A Third Virtue: Practical Wisdom

Had you known Lincoln before he was president, you would not have been surprised that he would deliver an excellent inaugural address. He had done that sort of thing before. He could also be expected to be deeply conscientious about taking the oath. He was, after all, Honest Abe, a deeply conscientious man. But that was Monday. You would not have known how he could handle what he had to do on Tuesday. Neither would Lincoln.

One passage of exceptional interest in the biography that would one day be written by two young men who not only worked but also lived in the White House deals with the tentativeness of relationships within the cabinet and with Lincoln in those first days. "The recognition and establishment of intellectual rank is difficult and slow. Perhaps the first real question of the Lincoln cabinet was, Who is the greatest man? It is safe to assert that no one—not even he himself—believed it was Abraham Lincoln."[16]

I said previously that Lincoln transformed the office and the office transformed him. The politician from the provinces, who had never been an executive of anything larger than a two-man law firm, who had never fired anyone, and who mocked his own military service in the state militia by reference to his bloody battle with mosquitoes and his attack on wild onions, was now, suddenly, the head of state, the executive, and commander-in-chief of the armed services in the greatest crisis in the nation's history.

He had not been a governor. He had not been a general. He had not been the head of a great department. He had been a politician, a lawyer, a legislator for a time, a political organizer, and a debater and maker of speeches. His address on Inauguration Day showed clarity and at the end a new eloquence, but the eloquence he achieved in the last paragraph on March 4 would not be what was needed on March 5. Could he make decisions? Could he lead? Did he have the ability to apply his principles to concrete cases that the ancients called prudence? Did he have practical wisdom and executive force?

Another president, Woodrow Wilson, had a very earnest Presbyterian sense of duty and also could make eloquent speeches stating large moral ideals. When he went to Europe to negotiate after the Great War, however, other questions arose. One young American, a realistically minded pastor of a little church in Detroit, reading about President Wilson in Europe, would write in his journal, "Wilson is a typical son of the manse. He believes too much in words. The sly Clemenceau [the realistic French premier] sneaks new meanings into these nice words."[17] Would Lincoln, who was also good with words, also believe in them too much?

The great economic thinker John Maynard Keynes described the huge letdown when Wilson went to Europe after the Great War:

> The President's program for the world, as set forth in his speeches and his notes, had displayed a spirit and a purpose so admirable that the last desire of his sympathizers was to criticize details—details, they felt, were quite right....

But in fact the President had thought out nothing; when it came to practice, his ideas were nebulous and incomplete. He had no plan, no scheme, no constructive ideas whatever for clothing with the flesh of life the commandments he had thundered from the White House. He could have preached a Sermon on any of them, or to have addressed a stately prayer to the Almighty for their fulfillment, but he could not frame their concrete application to the actual state of Europe.[18]

Lincoln could present his own, less Presbyterian, equivalents to Wilson's thundering sermons and stately prayers, but could he connect his moral ideas to a decision about the beleaguered fort in Charleston harbor? The equivalents of the "actual state of Europe" to which he had to apply his great principles were the last-ditch situation at Fort Sumter in the foreground and, in the background, secession of seven states and spreading rebellion.

And he had to face those issues right away. This president was to have absolutely no honeymoon. In the first business munute of his presidency he was slapped in the face by the necessity to make a decision of the utmost gravity: "'The first thing that was handed to me after I entered this room, when I came from the inauguration,' Lincoln would say, 'was the letter from Maj. Anderson saying that their provisions would be exhausted before an expedition could be sent to their relief.'"[19]

All nine officers who shared command at Sumter concurred. Lincoln learned from Maj. Robert Anderson's letter that the Confederates had so ringed the fort with threatening fortifications as to make it now impossible to relieve his little garrison with anything less than a force of "twenty thousand good and well disciplined men."[20] The entire Union Army, much of which was scattered in Indian posts in the West, then numbered only seventeen thousand.

What should an unmilitary new president, only a few hours into his presidency, do with this astounding communication? Obviously, he should call on the best available military advice—General-in-Chief Winfield Scott, one of the large figures of American military history. General Scott gave his opinion. There was nothing to be done but surrender the fort.

And what did Lincoln do? In the summary of these events that he would present later to Congress there would be a significant little editorial alteration that would obscure a huge presidential decision. After writing that General Scott concurred with Major Anderson in the view that Sumter must be evacuated, Lincoln wrote in the draft of the next sentence, "At the request of the Executive, however, he [meaning Scott] took full time," consulted with others, and thought it over some more.[21]

Hastily editing this document under the pressure of events in late June, Lincoln struck out the phrase "at the request of the executive" and substituted "on reflection," which made it sound as though General Scott had done the reflecting that caused him to draw back, take "full time," confer with others, and consider the matter again. But it was not Scott's reflection that caused the drawing back and reconsideration, it was Lincoln's: "at the request of the Executive." The fact that the newly arrived amateur turned aside a decision that all the old professionals had virtually already made was an immense determination. Lincoln had the independence and self-possession on his very first day to reject the advice to evacuate Fort Sumter.

He would do it again. After "consulting with other officers, both of the Army and the Navy," four days later Scott "came reluctantly, but decidedly, to the same conclusion as before."[22] General Scott this time even went so far as to submit to the president a letter, already composed, telling Major Anderson to withdraw. All it would have taken at that moment—less than a week into Lincoln's presidency—was his acceptance of that letter transmitting that order, ready to go. When Anderson notified Gen. P. G. T. Beauregard in Charleston Harbor that he was evacuating the fort, the chivalrous South Carolinians would have allowed the Union troops to have a little ceremony, lower the American flag, and withdraw. But again Lincoln made a mammoth decision that is shielded from the eyes of history because it was a decision *not* to act on advice being given. Lincoln did not permit Scott's letter to be sent.

Lincoln decided, and kept on deciding, *not* to evacuate Fort Sumter. Although a novice, he declined to do what his chief military officer, and all his top military officers, and his secretary of state, and the officers of the garrison in Fort Sumter itself, and originally the majority of the cabinet, together recommended. He wrote that military judgment was clear that the fort should be evacuated, but in his political judgment "to abandon that position would be utterly ruinous . . . that, in fact, it would be our national destruction consummated." His conclusion was a line in the sand: "This could not be allowed." So what to do?

Lincoln faced the intersection of two moral obligations. One was his solemn oath to "preserve, protect, and defend" the Union, to which end he promised to "hold, occupy and possess the property and places belonging to the Government," of which Fort Sumter was by all means the most important. The other moral obligation was his promise in his inaugural not to initiate armed conflict. To the "assailants of the Government" he had promised that "the Government will not assail you, unless you first assail it." He had written, "You can have no conflict without being yourselves the aggressors."

In this tight situation this novice president, this novice executive, would exhibit an unusual strategic imagination. He came to a masterful idea, a way to signify the Union's intention to "hold" and "possess" this most important government property and at the same time keep his promise not to initiate conflict. His plan had two parts, inextricably connected. First, the garrison needed bread, so send bread only, no arms. Second, notify the South Carolinians ahead of time that that was what you were doing.

After the Sumter expedition set forth, Lincoln sent a messenger to Gov. Francis Pickens of South Carolina, telling him that the expedition was bringing provisions only, no arms. Moreover, he had the first boat's pilot ready to deliver to any person opposing his entrance into Fort Sumter a further letter to be taken to Pickens that would explain the situation beyond all dispute. "The U.S. government has directed me [the pilot of the boat] to deliver a quantity of provisions to . . . Fort Sumter," the letter read, . . . "If your batteries open fire it will be upon an unarmed boat, and unarmed men performing an act of duty and humanity."

In his later summary of these events Lincoln would write that "the giving of bread to the few brave but starving men of the garrison, was all which would be attempted." On second thought, editing his draft, he apparently decided that "starving" might be overdoing it and substituted "hungry." Lincoln wanted the world to know that firing on the expedition would be "firing on bread for hungry men."

Whatever else advocates or scholars say about Sumter, his decision showed he could achieve practical wisdom in a tight spot. Nicolay and Hay give the result an extraordinary interpretation:

> When he finally gave the order that the fleet should sail he was master of the situation; master of his Cabinet; master of the moral attitude and issues of the struggle; master of the public opinion which must arise out of the impending conflict; master if the rebels hesitated or repented, because they would thereby forfeit their prestige with the South; master if they persisted, for he would then command a united North. And all this was done, it must be remembered, not in the retirement which gives calm reflection, but after the rush and hurry of a triumphal journey and the parade of an inauguration, in the confusion of conflicting counsel, the worry of preliminary appointments, the prevalence of an atmosphere of treason and insurrection, and the daily defection of Government officials.[23]

A Fourth Virtue: Union-saving Statecraft

Under the pressure of events, Lincoln would find in himself an extraordinary executive capacity. As he described the basis for the actions he took after Sumter, "It was with deepest regret that the Executive found the duty [this was a duty] of employing the war power, in defense of the government, forced upon him [it was not a free choice, but forced upon him]. He could but perform this duty [duty, again], or surrender the existence of the government."[24]

The last phrase is one instance of many in which Lincoln set forth his stark understanding of the stakes in the conflict. A victory by the rebels would be "the surrender of the existence of the government." Lincoln did not hold that benign view of secession implied in the outlook of Confederates then, of neo-Confederate Lincoln-haters now, and also of some antislavery folk then, who said "Let the erring sisters go." It was a benign view that would see some detachable units depart in peace, a graceful withdrawal, and then the Union, somewhat diminished in size, would sail on through history as before. Not at all.

Lincoln used the following verbs, nouns, and phrases to describe the effect of the rebellion's success: *surrender, destruction, immediate dissolution, our national destruction consummated, go to pieces, broken up, fall into ruin, the early destruction of our national Union, abandon, overthrow, not survive,* and *perish.* The entity that would be destroyed, surrendered, abandoned, dissolved, broken up, overthrown, and fall into ruin was variously and interchangeably described as the government, the Union, and the nation.

In the super-power days in the century to come, those who thought about high-level foreign policy would take over from European diplomatic thinkers the term *national interest* and fairly often modify it with the intensifier *vital.* But the interests they called "vital national interests" were rarely actually anywhere near vital. The nations in question would not die. In Lincoln's view the issue in the Civil War was truly vital. The success of the rebellion would mean that the American Union would not be just diminished, damaged, or (as in the Lincoln joke) "hurt pretty bad."[25] It would be dead. Destroyed.

In Lincoln's view, the rebellion put at risk not merely a part or aspect or few removable units of the Republic but its very life, existence, and essence. If one asks why in Lincoln's view it would have had so deep and crucial an effect, one can find the answers spelled out by Lincoln himself in the two great productions of 1861, the message to the Special Session and the Inaugural. If one asks to whom it would matter if the American Republic were destroyed, Lincoln would give the answer in the first interpretive paragraph, after he had recounted the history, of his first composition as president, the message to the Special Session on July 4, 1861:

And this issue [immediate dissolution or blood] embraces more than the fate of these United States. It presents to the whole family of man, the question, whether a constitutional republic, or a democracy—a government of the people, by the same people—can, or cannot maintain its territorial integrity, against its own domestic foes. It presents the question, whether discontented individuals, too few in numbers to control administration . . . can . . . break up their Government, and . . . put an end to free government upon the earth.[26]

Or, as he was to put it more elegantly and succinctly on a famous occasion later on, whether "government of the people, by the people, and for the people" should "perish from the earth."

The American Civil War was for Lincoln thus a unique event that threatened the life of the United States of America and popular government worldwide. It is important to underscore that uniqueness when Lincoln is used as a pattern and justification for the actions of other presidents or attacked as a tyrant who damaged civil liberty. As the distinguished Lincoln scholar Don E. Fehrenbacher wrote, "Makers of the modern 'imperial presidency' have drawn heavily on the example and immortal fame of Abraham Lincoln for vindication of their actions, conveniently ignoring the extent to which precedents taken from the Civil War are rendered invalid by its uniqueness. It is accordingly possible to conclude that Lincoln's use of executive power was wise and appropriate in its context, but not an unmixed blessing as a presidential tradition."[27]

For the purpose of identifying some of Lincoln's presidential virtues it is necessary to underscore his use of executive power as "wise and appropriate" and "eminently sound" in a situation that was indeed unique. Its uniqueness appears not only in the depth of general threat to the nation as Lincoln perceived it but also in specific situations. It is difficult indeed for a citizen of the twenty-first century to credit the danger that Lincoln and the nation confronted during the first days of his presidency. The attacks on Pearl Harbor and on the World Trade Center were powerful shocks, but neither the Japanese and the Axis in 1941 nor jihadists in 2001 had the power to overthrow the secure super power the United States had become. Lincoln described the situation of the nation's capital, which the Founders situated in a swamp between two slave states, in April of 1861: "all the roads and avenues to this city were obstructed, and the capital was put into the condition of a siege. The mails in every direction were stopped, and the lines of telegraph cut off by the insurgents, and military and naval forces, which had been called out by the government for the defense of Washington, were prevented from reaching the city."[28]

In the terrible last weeks of April, when mobs in Baltimore stopped Union troops from reaching Washington and a committee of fifty men from the Baltimore YMCAs called on him to urge that he sent no more troops through Baltimore, Lincoln responded, mentioning again his oath: "The rebels attack

Fort Sumter, and your citizens attack troops sent to the defense of the Government, and the lives and property in Washington, and yet you would have me break my oath and surrender the Government without a blow. There is no Washington in that—no Jackson in that—no manhood or honor in that."[29]

He undertook an extraordinary series of actions, some of which, as he put it, "were without any authority of law."[30] He called for volunteers, proclaimed a blockade of southern ports, increased the size of the army and navy, authorized the spending of public funds by private citizens, and suspended the writ of habeas corpus in certain areas. As Lincoln described his choice, "It became necessary for me to choose whether, using only the existing means, agencies, and processes which Congress had provided, I should let the government fall at once into ruin, or whether, availing myself of the broader powers conferred by the Constitution in cases of insurrection, I would make an effort to save it with all its blessings for the present age and for posterity."[31] He chose the latter, and what resulted was, he said, that "the government was saved from overthrow."

During the next four years he would exhibit practical wisdom and executive skill in a myriad of ways. He demonstrated that he could relate his large moral idea to the demands and the limitations of particular concrete situations. This president could make up his mind. He did not procrastinate or dither. He was willing to make hard and painful decisions. He had clarity of mind and resolution. He had shown firmness against all compromises with secessionists in the winter before he came to office, and in contrast to his predecessor he would show strong will in the enormous decisions he made during the first four months in office.

He would show steadfast resolution in prosecuting the war and in one dark period produced a sentence remarkable for its moral rigor, literary grace, and lawyerly covering of all contingencies: "I expect to maintain this contest until successful, or 'till I die, or am conquered, or my term expires, or Congress or the country forsakes me."[32]

He could take strong action forthrightly, as he would do to keep Maryland in the Union. But he could also exercise sensitive restraint and shrewdness, as he would do in keeping Kentucky in the Union. He could admit he was wrong and admit mistakes, as he would do in his remarkable letters to generals, particularly to Ulysses S. Grant, and he could change course, as he would do with respect to emancipation. His strength of will was grounded not in ego or stubbornness but in strength of mind.

What one chooses to praise in someone else can be revealing. When in 1852 Lincoln eulogized his first political hero, Henry Clay, he said Clay had an "indomitable will." But Clay, said Lincoln, also had good judgment. Without that good judgment, Lincoln said, an indomitable will can be "nothing better than . . . useless obstinacy."[33] Strength of mind was the grounding of Lincoln's own strength of will.

A Fifth Virtue: Treating Equality as the Nation's Premise

Usually the most important single criterion for appraising a president is the direction of policy he represents. On that point Lincoln was, to borrow his own figure, facing toward Zion. He rose to prominence by his ability to relate the moral condemnation of the "monstrous injustice" of slavery to the practical political situation. He was, from the start, a spokesperson for a large moral idea, a nation grounded in the Declaration of Independence.

That idea did not vanish when he became president. It is often said that the American Civil War was fought at the start as a power struggle, merely to defend the Union, and only with the Emancipation Proclamation became something larger, a war for universal moral principle. For Lincoln, there was an immense moral issue from the beginning: the fate of republican government.

There was a social and an economic dimension to it. Lincoln said in that first presidential message that the Union was fighting to maintain "that form and substance of government, whose leading object is, to elevate the condition of men—to lift artificial weights from all shoulders—to clear the paths of laudable pursuit for all—to afford all, an unfettered start, and a fair chance, in the race of life."[34] It fought, that is, for a principle of both universal moral worth in itself and the ground on which slavery would be condemned. Those shoulders from which weights would be lifted—all shoulders—would for Lincoln include, although he would not make it explicit perhaps even to himself and certainly not to his listeners, the shoulders of black men.

Lincoln had a six-year track record, after all, that made clear his moral judgment of slavery; the Republican Party had an identity. Lincoln had, as Phillip Paludan has written, "integrated the premises of equality within a commitment to the constitutional process. . . . The Union that Buchanan and Pierce led certainly would have preserved slavery for the foreseeable future. But Lincoln had been arguing for many years that the Democrats' perception of the nature and meaning of the Union was wrong. . . . Lincoln's challenge to slavery was already in existence in 1861."[35]

During secession winter, while South Carolina and six other states were seceding, members of Congress scrambled to compromise, but President-elect Lincoln out in Springfield scotched any compromise that added new territory for slavery and insisted that nothing be done that implied slavery was on a moral par with freedom. In an exchange of letters with his old Whig congressional colleague Alexander Stephens, now vice president of the Confederacy, Stephens made clear from his side that Georgia and the other states could not remain in a Union that had as its premise that slavery was wrong. Lincoln made clear from his side that the Union as he understood it could never yield on that point.

Lincoln had made the egalitarian premise of the Declaration of Independence, specifically including black persons, the centerpiece of his years-long argument with Stephen Douglas, and that premise was for him part of the meaning of the constitutional Union. When he made large statements of inclusive national ideals—like the one about weights from all shoulders, clearing the path for all, and affording all an unfettered start and fair chance—he was implicitly including blacks.

His large statements of the moral ideals of which the United States was the bearer—like this one—had latent within their implications the eventual ending and present disapproval of slavery. The next sentences in this paragraph in the message to the Special Session indicate again, in a backhanded way, that the eventual ending of slavery was part of Lincoln's concept of the Union's moral meaning. "Yielding to partial, and temporary departures, from necessity," wrote President Lincoln to Congress, "this [the "unfettered fair start for all"] is the leading object of the government for whose existence we contend."[36] What can he have meant by that preliminary concession about temporary partial yieldings to necessity, except his position on slavery? We must accept it in the states where it exists but only by necessity and only temporarily, not on principle and not forever.

The moral purpose of Lincoln's war at the beginning was not yet explicitly "a new birth of freedom." It was to preserve, maintain, defend, and prevent destruction of the old, but "the old" in Lincoln's terms, the Republican Party's terms. The old government that the Union fought to maintain had, for Lincoln, an ideal and an aspirational content from which a new birth of freedom would one day spring.

A Sixth Virtue: Morality without Self-righteousness

In his personal ethic Lincoln managed to combine resolution with charity, a difficult combination. In one letter he gave often-quoted expressions of both. As to his resolution, he asked, "What would you do in my position? Would you drop the war where it is? Or, would you prosecute it in . . . with elder-stalk squirts, charged with rose water? Would you deal lighter blows rather than heavier ones? Would you give up the contest, leaving any available means unapplied?" But then after a short intervening paragraph he wrote one of his most notable expressions of charity, of magnanimity, that adds something even to the Second Inaugural: "I shall do nothing in malice. What I deal with is too vast for malicious dealing."[37] If we did a full treatment of Lincoln's virtues we would deal at length with his magnanimity, his not holding grudges, his not seeking revenge.

Alongside his personal ethic there was his social ethic. Lincoln's great distinction as the leader of the nation in a giant war would be that even though he understood the struggle to have a moral shape, and even though he saw the stakes to be immense, and even though he pursued victory in that war with great resolution through many disappointments, he did so in a profound way that avoided turning the war into a moralistic melodrama.

He spoke of evil—slavery as a vast moral evil—but did not locate the evil exclusively among those he opposed. Nor did he absolve his own side. Lincoln did not require moral simplicism in order to be resolute. He achieved moral force without self-righteousness and moral clarity the other side of complexity rather than on this side of it. Lincoln would often use explicit moral language, and he would do so in a carefully formulated and thoughtful way that avoided the perils of self-righteousness and moralizing oversimplification.[38] He would be an unmoralistic moralist.

A Seventh Virtue: Religious Profundity

If any other president had been speaking in the situation in which Lincoln gave his Second Inaugural address listeners would have expected triumphalism. With Lincoln, they heard something very different. As he had said throughout so he said again: Slavery was an offense of the whole nation. The references to God by this one-time scoffer who never joined a church would be unique in two ways. First, they developed over time. Second, they did not identify the purposes of God with his own side in battle. Can those things be said of any other wartime president—or peacetime president either, for that matter?

The distinctive elements of the Second Inaugural began to appear after the war had gone on longer than he, or anyone else, had anticipated and casualty lists stretched far beyond anyone's forecast. He was able to combine moral seriousness with self-criticism by understanding his actions as only part of a vast historical drama whose outcome neither he nor his adversaries wholly determined but which nevertheless had moral meaning.

When a modern president said that Lincoln "believed in the Almighty" and showed "you have to be a religious person to be a great president" it did not seem to be an adequate account of the one-time scoffer who bypassed conventional piety on both sides and became our greatest president.[39] When he was in his early twenties, Lincoln read Tom Paine, memorized Robert Burns's satire on smug Presbyterians, and wrote a scorcher about religious orthodoxy so shocking his friends did him the favor of burning it. As he advanced in politics he put aside scoffing and displayed knowledge of the King James Bible and sometimes the deeper reaches of Christian ethics that went beyond that of many church members—without becoming one himself.

When a modern president said that believing in the Almighty made Lincoln, even in hard times, "optimistic," the comment seemed a little too easy. Consider a remarkable passage from Lincoln's most remarkable speech: "Fondly do we hope, fervently do we pray, that this mighty scourge of war may speedily pass away. Yet, if God wills that it continue until all the wealth piled by the bondman's two-hundred and fifty years of unrequited toil shall be sunk, and until every drop of blood drawn with the lash shall be paid by another drawn with the sword, as was said three thousand years ago, so still it must be said, 'The judgments of the Lord are true and righteous altogether.'" To call that passage "optimistic" would be to call the ocean a pond.

It is usually the case that references to God have the effect of trying to play a transcendent trump card for one's own side, but Lincoln's opened the story to a larger dimension than either side comprehended. He specifically and explicitly set God's controlling Providence against, even in contrast to, the purposes of the contending parties, including his own. The pivotal sentence is, "The Almighty has His Own purposes."[40]

3. Lincoln Spoils the War

MARK W. SUMMERS

Those love her best, who to themselves are true.
And what they dare to dream of, dare to do.
—James Russell Lowell, "Ode Recited at the
Harvard Commemoration"

The invasion of Washington, D.C., early in March 1861 took nobody by surprise. Everyone had expected aggressive moves from the invading force since Election Day. Newspapers had given generous space to the mustering of hosts, the strategic advantages of adversaries, and the objectives of the top commanders. Nothing in the annals of war could match the determination of the most ardent volunteers. The slaughter, as everybody agreed, would be colossal. Indeed, few among those faithful few standing firm at their posts expected anything better than that the enemy would wipe them out to the last man. By every reckoning, Washington had not seen so brutal a struggle in four years.

But then every president had the same experience. Every time one administration went out and another came in, the city was put under siege from office-seekers and deserving partisans. All federal offices became part of the spoils of war, fit for grabbing.[1] Long before a soldier rallied against the Union's enemies in the field the Lincoln administration was fending off the usual onslaught of its friends in the foyer, one and all clamoring for the places and perquisites that by right victors always claimed.

A daunting noise this clamor and cackle from spoils-hunters makes just at the start of the Civil War. But then feeding time at the zoo amid the blast of bugles and the thunder of cavalry steeds never takes on the timbre of romance. Nothing spoils a war quite so much as breaking from it for the war over spoils. Naturally, historians have left this topic pretty much alone.[2] Actions deserving the Purple Heart will always be likelier to earn the purple prose.

Still, the scramble is worth pausing to observe, however briefly, if only because raw political maneuvering tells us things we should not overlook about the Civil War, the limits in Abraham Lincoln's power to shape events as he would, and the persistence, even to our own day, of the two-party system.

The spoils system was older than the Union itself and, as far as the party faithful were concerned, nearly as sacred. Since Andrew Jackson's day thirty years before, office-brokering had been done much more overtly. When Sen. William Marcy of New York explained that his friends saw nothing wrong in the premise that to the victor belonged the spoils he was simply blurting out a distasteful truth.[3] No president fired everybody, certainly not all at once, but the axe hung poised over every clerk's head, and each administration let it fall more generally than the one before.[4] By the 1850s an official could promise only that he would decapitate underlings "in as kind and gentlemanly a manner as any man could do it, *and that ought to satisfy them if they are reasonable!*"[5] His fellow Democrats stood every chance of feeling the same "satisfaction." By the 1850s, officeholders trembled for their heads even when the government stayed in the same party's grip. From retirement Marcy grumbled that he may have spoken of letting the victors have the spoils; he had said nothing about plundering one's own camp![6]

Patronage was more than the reward for a political party winning office, although certainly it was that in ways more complicated than the quid pro quo for chivying the rank and file to the polls. Spoils meant wealth for a few lucky appointees.[7] For others it meant a supplement to their meager earnings as partisan editors. More important than spoils' use to express gratitude to *"working men"* for a job well done, they provided official recognition of the appointee's importance inside the party hierarchy and his sponsor's influence.[8]

Once a party leader had invested moral capital behind candidates, their rejection took on importance far beyond the benefits that the office and gratitude of its holder could convey. The whole party organization would be demoralized. Refuse his nominations, a Connecticut senator warned, and "my humiliation and disgrace will be complete." Choosing anyone else would injure the good cause and mete out "intense mortification." Furious on suspicion that their nominee to a diplomatic post in Italy would be turned down, Vermont's senators threatened to resign if not given their way.[9]

Done right, job-allotting defined precisely how strong one faction in a party was compared to another and hinted at what larger preferment the applicant could expect at the party's hands in the future. Handing out the goodies inspired future good service from beneficiaries and was an example for up-and-coming partisans of what honors might come their way if they kept political fealty.[10]

It sounds sordid—at least when the opposing party did it. But what was the alternative? In the days before civil service examinations, hiring on the basis of merit, and an apolitical bureaucracy became the norm, elected officials could not afford to leave the machinery of government in the opposition's hands. Officeholders who had the wrong political view could halt or hamstring any program and, as usual, cough up a share of their salaries to add to the opposition's coffers, even day-laborers trundling wheelbarrows.[11] If policies were to be implemented, every postmaster, customs collector, and official printer would need to work for the administration, and the sooner "the present, immediate, active & unflinching influence of clear-headed, strong-willed, true-hearted and wise Republicans" bore down on the paperwork, the better![12] Why should Democratic newspapers fatten on postal receipts and government advertising when they used their gains to mislead the public further about what Republicans meant to do? Patronage was not separate from policy; it was the first step in making that policy possible. Resenting something so natural verged on bad taste, even among the victims. "Wherever the President can work his ax, let him work it," a Kentucky senator exclaimed. "Let him take off their heads; let him put in his men; and I, for one, never have complained, and never will complain."[13]

We may imagine that war would have changed the basic rules of political combat. Surely, politics should have taken a furlough for the duration. For all the high-sounding insistence that the only two parties now were patriots and traitors, however, neither Republicans nor Democrats had the slightest intention of dropping their guard for long. A Peace Democrat, Clement Vallandigham, said it precisely when he declared that war was just politics with bayonets and that politics was war without the bayonets.[14] A two-party system might well make a healthy check on the ravening hunger for power that wars always stimulate, but that was a case for political scientists to make later on rather than for stump-speakers to make at the time. Republicans thundered that Democrats, by existing at all, were aiding the enemy. Senate and House were honeycombed with conspirators and traitors—or at any rate critics of the administration, which amounted to the same thing.[15] Those leading the host into war were bigger than party. They were the People's Will, fending off that miserable faction mantled in a party label it no longer deserved and at best serving as an expression of the People's Won't. Under the circumstances, putting none but loyal men on guard mattered now more than ever, and that meant making Democratic clerks a going concern.

That did not make the shambles in the first days of the Lincoln administration any less appalling. To play on the most famous words the Great Emancipator never said, God must have loved the office-seekers, He made so many of them. The winning Republican coalition had endless components, and each expected recognition not only for what it was but also for what it once had been.[16] "What a run, what a race for offices," Count Adam Gurowski marveled as he watched the crowds descend on the capital. "Some of the party leaders seem to me similar to children enjoying a long-expected and ardently wished for toy. . . . [No] one seems to look over Mason and Dixon's line to the terrible and with lightning-like velocity spreading fire of hellish treason."[17] "I am sick and nauseated with this miserable, selfish clamoring for appointment to office," Sen. James R. Doolittle of Wisconsin raged. "I sometimes wish I had never recommended a man." But he had, did, and kept on doing so. A year later he gathered the entire Wisconsin delegation behind one ticket for every single new assessor and collector's office in the state and demanded that they be put through wholesale. Lincoln did so eagerly, if only to escape pestering from Wisconsin at least.[18]

Nothing could change the fact that the administration needed to rely on its friends for its success. Republicans bristled at the suggestion that emptying the offices could wait a few months. Democrats were just plain greedy, Sen. Lyman Trumbull of Illinois snarled. The enemy had "his officers fattening, and thinks they are not yet in good condition." Republicans were not about to let them hold on and "catch the crumbs that are to fall from the public crib."[19] So, out went Democrats and in came the faithful. The president appointed 1,639 offices himself, and incumbents lost their heads in well over a thousand of them.[20] Democrats at the Philadelphia arsenal were quizzed about whom they would vote for, and a week after the off-year elections in 1862 each was handed a dismissal note.[21]

We should not assume from this that appointments were only on the basis of party service any more than every appointment meant removal. Appointees quit, retired, and died. The Boston and Philadelphia customshouses might draw party lines tight, whereas New York's collector left about half the Democrats where they had been—one reason he was removed before Lincoln's first term came to an end.[22] A saving remnant of Democrats who had vital expertise survived the war unsacked. A Democratic record could actually help an applicant for promotion—especially when it came to choosing generals.

The more responsible the position asked, the more a letter of recommendation had to stress the applicants' talents or at least good character.[23] When the secretary of the treasury justified his choices for assessor and collector by declaring the nominee the best for the service it was a repetition as meaningless as a conversational How are you?—especially because he rarely troubled to explain how an applicant's credentials better fitted him for the responsibilities of the post.[24] But the bow to efficiency had to be made.

Partisan devotion could put an aspirant in, but no amount of political grandstanding could keep him there long. Even so highly placed a politician as Simon Cameron, by all odds the once and future boss of the Republican Party in Pennsylvania, lasted a little under a year in the War Department before his shortcomings eased him out into diplomatic service. If he ended as minister to Russia it may have been only because there was no vacancy further away to which the administration could send him.

Under Edwin M. Stanton, Cameron's successor, the War Department put efficiency before political preferment, and Stanton was no mere watchdog on spending. He was more a bloodhound, ferocious on the trail of wastrels and peculators. Lincoln's aides may not have been the only people in Washington who would rather have come down with a case of smallpox than ask Stanton for a favor. That efficiency, however, made the secretary irreplaceable. His devotion to the service made him just about fireproof—or firing-proof.[25]

Wartime patronage hunting did not breed a worse saturnalia than usual. Compared to James Buchanan's presidency or Ulysses Grant's, Lincoln's appointees were a relatively honest lot. Only the jump in spending allowed a member of Congress from Massachusetts to claim that the Treasury had been robbed of more in a single year of Lincoln's regime than "the entire current yearly expenses of the Government" under his predecessor.[26] Only a Democrat would believe that one contractor had been arrested and hurled into Fort Lafayette's rankest dungeon cell for putting in too low a bid.[27]

Scandals there were, however, especially among military suppliers chosen for political pull rather than the ability to do the job. It was strictly true, as a critic charged, that "the blood of our men, the groans of our wounded, the tears of the orphan and the wail of the widow, have been coined into money."[28] The Republicans' motto, their enemies sneered, was "if this be treason, we'll make the most of it," and Democrats suggested that the real snake in the grass in the administration was not the much-mentioned Anaconda strategy but the boa contractor. More pervasive was the wide array of appointees apparently chosen to prove that anybody could do the job. With some justice a Democrat nailed home how little he knew about military matters by swearing that he was "as profoundly ignorant . . . as any brigadier general . . . recently appointed."[29] One might suggest that Lincoln's creation of a national Thanksgiving Day was all the more fitting surrounded as he was by so many gobblers.

And yet the war turned out none the worse for the spoliators and spoilers. Indeed, it is quite possible that the way that Lincoln applied the spoils, and the fact that he had them to apply worked to his advantage. The disharmonies of the federal government at their worst were never as bitter as those that marred Jefferson Davis's Confederate authority. Cantankerous objections and cankering resentment added more than a touch of ineffectuality to the decrees coming out of Richmond. The were many reasons, of course, including the lack of partisan affiliation among southern governors, whereas Republican fealty made most northern ones active in helping Lincoln do what needed to be done—often sooner than he was prepared to do it; the differences in personality between Lincoln and Davis; and the harrowing effect of defeat and retreat for inspiring endless recrimination. Davis lacked the tools and certainly the skill in awarding offices that allowed him to satisfy party organizations. There were no parties. Where jobs were not allotted according to the ideal, the most capable candidate, they went to oblige politicians who had the most pull. "Every body wants office," a diarist noted, "and every body raises an outcry at the corruption of those who get the offices." Wherever their loyalty lay, officers felt no special allegiance to Davis. Under the Confederate constitution, he could not dismiss them on political grounds, and he had no personal reason to demand their service. Fundamental law made him ineligible for re-election. There was no way that the Confederate president could have applied jobs as Lincoln did, to turn away wrath.[30]

And he did turn away wrath, which, in view of the past and future history of how the spoils system worked, was a positive miracle. For once, patronage did not set the party by the ears, with faction mauling faction and all of them sharing in a disappointment with the administration. It was an astonishing anomaly! Patronage politics at mid-century, with no other exception, tore gaping holes in whatever party had the spoils at its disposal. Tyler, Polk, Taylor, Fillmore, Pierce, and Buchanan each set off vicious in-fighting and bred election-year disasters by the way he disposed of loaves and fishes. In every administration at least one major appointment served as a fireship to set the entire party ablaze.[31] The familiar story would repeat itself, if in milder form, under the three postwar presidents, not to mention with James A. Garfield, who fulfilled the spoils system's highest possibilities by devoting his entire administration to a quarrel over the New York customshouse and died that summer at the hands of a disappointed office-seeker.[32]

All in all, one might conclude that most presidents should have found patronage more trouble politically than it was worth. Among the discouraging line of presidential misadventures Lincoln alone seems to have escaped nearly unscathed. The Republican Party ended the war consolidated, entrenched, and, as far as majority parties could be, harmonious and intermittently united. How had he done it? Or had he done it at all?

Lincoln did plenty to make patronage run more smoothly, but the system itself, as it was developing, helped. Over time, an etiquette had developed that was complicated but universally accepted. Republican members of Congress should be consulted about appointments in their districts; if a Democrat held the seat, the local party organization—the committee, usually, or its chair—had a compelling say.[33]

It made sense, in a way. As the number of offices expanded, presidents, cabinet officers, and even senators could not possibly think of enough apt names to fill the places. As the national government's responsibilities increased and the president's duties cut into the six-month vacations that a John Adams could enjoy, department heads did not have time to study the specific needs of Republicans in, say, Peewee Valley. They needed to consult those closest to the local constituencies. Greater knowledgeability carried greater power, however, and far from growing imperial with so many more jobs to pass out presidents found themselves restricted in whom they could put where. Woe to any member of Congress who meddled with who got a post office in someone else's district! And woe to any president who picked an outsider or a man unconnected with the local machine for an office that Congress every year treated as its own private preserve! Not long before the war, a reporter described one persnickety lawmaker as behaving like a wrathful diner in a Manhattan chophouse, shouting at the president, "Waiter, there! Fitch us up two half-dozen postmasters on a hard shell, and a dozen light-houses, d'ye mind? Waiter! Is it twice I am to call?—me, the representative of one hundred thousand people? Is it a beggar ye take me for?"[34] By now it seemed as if everyone on Capitol Hill was like that.

Other offices had too wide an influence for local control or helped feed neighboring states, where the pickings were comparatively slim. Connecticut and New Jersey politicians expected a share in the swag that the Brooklyn Navy Yard distributed, and those in New Hampshire would wax wroth if left out of the drippings from the Boston customshouse. The fattest plums—collectors of the port, for instance—depended on a senator's say. Any of the larger offices at a president's disposal that entailed confirmation needed senatorial acquiescence or the rest of the senators would band together to defeat the nomination.[35] Territorial offices and diplomatic appointments usually were apportioned among the states, and it was expected that a fair balance would be worked out. New York and Pennsylvania could not have hogged those jobs even if the War Department was in the hands of one and the State Department in the hands of the other.[36] In all these matters the president's ability to nominate as he chose was hemmed in tightly. But then the more hemmed in he was, the less flak he took for whatever choices he made.

The system could not prevent some mishaps. Sometimes state officers wanted one slate of candidates and its members of Congress wanted another. Senators might disagree about who should fill an office vital to them both.[37]

When a cabinet officer was a major player in a state's politics, he claimed as his own right a say in who should be appointed, even when rivals on Capitol Hill demanded the final word as a matter of senatorial courtesy. In quarrels like those the president's discretionary authority widened considerably.

Those clashes, though, were more rare than they might have been because Republicans had devised a mechanism for making sure that control over appointments lay firmly with Congress. An entire state delegation would meet and agree on a slate of candidates rather than ask for nominees in a piecemeal fashion. The slate allowed trade-offs to be made so factions could all receive something solid in return for making concessions. There would be no pie today for one side on the promise of pie some day for the others. A slate that had unanimous approval from a delegation made the administration an offer it could not refuse—or at least not without angering the state organization. A president could not play one senator against another; indeed, he put himself at risk even by modest fiddling with the list of names. A delegation's unity depended on the all-or-nothing quality of the slate. Cooperating from the first, members of Congress from a state could hardly complain about being left in the cold once they had got their way. Moreover, they could hardly blame the president for choosing wrong when the choice was the united request of a delegation.[38]

The president knew how far the patronage game was a matter of recognition and not solid preferment. Highly placed politicians wanted to show supporters that they had access as much as they wanted to show off the offices they had acquired. No one could get everything or expected his member of Congress to take every trick. Lincoln would consult officers and lawmakers hard before making a decision and make it clear that, far from coming up with the name of a suitable appointee, he had drawn upon the names presented to him and weighed the relative strengths of their backers. He would also regularly write a note on letters of recommendation. At the least it was a token of his personal interest in the case, and more often than not it was friendly interest. Of course, the department heads knew well that there were finely graded levels of support. If the president advised that the application be given attention, it meant he expected nothing more substantial than that.[39] A genial reminder that the supplicant was from New York and "very well recommended" implied no obligation to hire him, as in that particular case the secretary of state did not.[40] "Let it be fairly considered" might as well have been a peremptory "Devil take him."[41] A line or two urging the applicant's appointment, if practicable or consistent with the good of the service, allowed a secretary all the outs necessary to turn the applicant away gently.[42] A general comment that the president would like to do something for the sponsoring member of Congress made perfectly clear that this particular applicant could be rejected as long as some other compensation, somewhere, sometime later—perhaps much later—could be found for his backer.[43] Only rarely did the president insist that the appointment be made. When he said "let it be done," appointment was only days away, and confirmation was almost sure within the week.[44] To the officer doing the appointing, the precise words mattered. The fact that there were friendly words at all, however, may have weighed considerably more with the applicant and his powerful friends.

At the same time, Lincoln's conditional support worked in quite another way. By not insisting on his preferences for office the president left cabinet officers with wide discretion and a sense of their own broad authority—an ideal way of keeping them on good terms and letting them persuade themselves that they were kings in their own kitchen. Even the president's apparent demands were less than that. "You must make a job of it, and provide a place for the bearer of this," Lincoln instructed Philadelphia's director of the Mint. "Make a job of it with the Collector, and have it done. You can do it for me, and you must." The director did not, and two years later when the applicant finally had a place it was as the State Department's man in Laguara, Venezuela.[45] Effectively, he allowed them to build their own smaller patronage empires, shaping their preferences, if only slightly, to strengthen their prospects of reaching higher office in the future. But that power carried with it most of the blame when the wrong choices were made. When a request was denied the president could clear himself of responsibility. Whatever anger the rejected might have would direct itself at the department heads and, on the rare occasions when the president's intervention overrode the secretaries, redound all the more to his credit.

Lincoln also did his best to soften the blow of rejection when powerful sponsors were involved. He worked to find another office for applicants who had been turned down and tried to find ways of obliging members of Congress by giving them their way on one thing when he could not arrange it on the other. Sometimes he wrote to explain or apologize for his inability to do them a favor. Those letters were meant more as reassurance that they still had real clout with the administration and that good things yet would come. "It was with great regret that I felt constrained to give the tax appointment . . . to another," he wrote to Connecticut's miffed senior senator. "If some arrangement for his benefit could be made, I should be glad. I hope to find an opportunity of yet recognizing him."[46]

That interest showed itself in another way: the president's readiness to give lawmakers the small-change patronage that mattered to them most personally, appointment for sons, cousins, and in-laws. Illinois senator Lyman Trumbull had a son who wanted into the naval academy; the president made sure that it was done. Vermont's influential senior senator had a son who wanted a commission. That, too, the president arranged.[47] There were plenty of cousins and in-laws of his own who were given preferment, and, of course, cabinet officers found all sorts of berths for their kin. That, too, could not have happened without Lincoln's appreciation of family values in the most personal sense.

Factionalism, though, was more than a matter of one ambitious Lady Bountiful elbowing another aside. It had a sharp basis in principle. Republicans came in every shade, and some of them loathed each other to the point of imaginary homicide. Lincoln's talent for keeping ministering hands on the process while leaving the hard-knuckled fists to his underlings served him exceptionally well in keeping disputes over principle from growing even uglier by tangling them with strife over offices. For all the arguments that historians have had as to whether the president was a conservative or a radical, or, perhaps a conservative radical, a close inspection of his patronage policy gets no closer to an answer. The president played no favorites.

Radicals got patronage and so did conservatives. Democrats shared with Republicans, and old-line Free Soil members were as privileged as late-coming opportunists. It is conceivable that Charles Sumner's influence in Massachusetts could have been diminished to the advantage of his gentle colleague Henry Wilson or the far less radical former speaker of the House Nathaniel P. Banks. The latter was given a military command, but offices were passed out in the Bay State in ways that could make no harm for anyone. Ben Wade in Ohio had more fierce disagreements with the equally radical Salmon P. Chase than he did with the conservatives, but neither was there much complaint from conservative members of the party about being shut out of the spoils.[48]

Of course, each faction could have distributed patronage better than the president did, given a perfectly free hand. In the hours after Lincoln's assassination a group of radicals consoled themselves for the president's loss by parceling out the offices in the new Johnson administration and listing those cabinet officers whose retirement would be welcomed. They never got what they wanted, any more than the Democrats did, who were drawing up their own slates for a new assemblage of officeholders. It was only human nature for politicians to wish they had been bestowed with more than they got. "Take seven cats, put them together in a bag, sew up its mouth, and shake it up well—WELL, mind you," a senator scoffed, "and you have the Cabinet!"[49] The weakness was a strength when it came to each faction having at least some cat that would jump its way.

Thus the discontents were never so serious as to mar party success, and certainly they never proved fatal. In state after state the president's policy seemed to be that there was enough to go around and enough for all. Indeed, there very nearly was—or at least as far as insatiable appetites could ever have even so much as the edge taken off their hunger. For once, the feast was almost big enough, which in the peacetime world of severely limited government would have been unimaginable. The offices at the command of the government grew, as did the rewards that good Republicans could count on to help pay for the political machinery. In 1862, to take just one example, Congress created the Internal Revenue system. That entailed a host of commissioners and collectors, most of whom owed their careers to Congress. They repaid it in up-to-date information on political sentiment at the grass roots, in attendance directing party conventions, in subsidies for party newspapers, and help at election time. The Customs Service had existed since the founding of the Republic, but with the passage of the Morrill War Tariff receipts were far larger than before. The rake-off in fees and fines was considerably larger as well, and this, too, the Republican Party found ways of using. Clerks, bookkeepers, special Treasury agents, all these and more the war required the government to appoint where few or none had been needed before.

Then there was the crowd of military offices. Every general had sponsors, and promotion, transfer, and preferment were all fresh forms of patronage. Armies that marched on their stomachs moved ahead on their commissary officers and paymasters.[50] Order behind the front and in the recruiting of manpower in unheard-of numbers demanded a host of provost marshals. All constituted grist for the spoils system, and all allowed politicians to ask favors and prove their worth to the rank and file by their skill at delivering them.

The expansion of federal contracts and offices allowed those left out on the first helping to push forward, bowl in hand, for the second—or third. For those to whom civilian employment did not beckon there were opportunities to be, as Banks was, a general, slaking a thirst for glory. The scramble never ended, but that was one reason why the scramble may have left fewer Republicans unreconciled than might be otherwise.

Clearly, then, Lincoln used the spoils system in a masterful way, but neither genius or gentle touch alone explains his accomplishment. Special circumstances spared him the catastrophe that met other presidents on patronage matters.

It needs to be seen that most patronage fights in other administrations mingled with intense disagreements over policy. Job hunting made disputes worse and more ill-tempered, but the disputes were there to begin with. The quarrel over offices under Buchanan would have been a minor grievance had it not come over an issue that to many northern Democrats ranked as politically vital—whether the people of Kansas, willy-nilly, should be forced to accept a constitution imposing slavery on the prospective state. The quarrel that Grant's administration raised was not just over who he lavished offices upon but the principle that a public office should not be a private hustle. Those who complained the loudest were alarmed at other symptoms of the same selfish spirit: the protective tariff, the subsidies and land grants to privileged railroad corporations, and the push to annex Santo Domingo, apparently to gratify the appetites of speculators who had high political connections.[51] Differences over issues counted far more than spats over spoils, and patronage was especially divisive when no one wanted to bring up present issues. When spoils were the only thing to talk about they became important enough to break heads over.

None of these conditions applied to Civil War America. The spoils system should remind us that for all the talk of politics having adjourned, partisanship persisted; peacetime habits were interrupted briefly during the first shock after Fort Sumter but revitalized by summertime. Republicans called for a union movement in which the two parties joined forces, but what they really wanted was a larger Republican Party under whatever new name—People's or Union Party—it could be fashioned. Democrats would be given prominent places on the speaker's stand and not quite as often on the ticket, but with the hopes that the converts would stay when peace arrived. The idea that federal offices would be handed out without regard to party affiliation was not even considered. The notion that the newspaper deserving to publish the official government advertising should be the one with the largest circulation, as opposed to that run by a needy Republican editor, was too outlandish to go very far.

If anything, the war reinforced and intensified partisan differences. "Every dog that wags his tongue against the integrity of the Union must be slain," a general shouted to one party audience.[52] Branded as traitors and defeat-mongers, the Democrats insisted that Republicans were the true fanatics, enemies of liberty, and something very separate from the true patriots they were themselves.[53] No terms of peace would erase their memory of that fact. What ground could Democrats share with ranters who shouted for "Subjugation, Confiscation, Emancipation, Expurgation, and Emigration" or threatened the Supreme Court? What share of the spoils could blind them to scattered type in the streets from newspaper presses smashed by Republican mobs or to war critics tarred, feathered, and ridden out of town on a rail?[54] The slights, the slurs that in wartime set Republicans apart from Democrats, would be remembered for generations, well into the adulthood of voters born after the war ended.[55] The "bloody shirt" became the surest way of galvanizing political opinion and driving partisans to the polls, north and south. Generals pointed to their honorable scars to win office, and both parties pointed to the scars that the war had put upon the country and, as Democrats would have it, its Constitution, as justification for renewed and constant support.

The war set traitors against traitors—at least in each other's view. Republicans might differ strongly. They might see themselves as "earnest men" in clear contrast to allies whose soul lacked the requisite ideological iron.[56] They might fear "fanatics" in their midst or deride the weak and fainthearted. For the most part, however, they could tell friends from outright foes and knew that however far a Charles Sumner and an Orville Browning might differ in politics their differences were infinitesimal compared to those they had with the party of treason and Clement Vallandigham.[57]

Disagree though they might, Republicans shared one firm conviction: Only by war could the Union be restored or at any rate a Union worth keeping and living in and meant to last. Democrats shared no such conviction, and many of them, as time went on, sounded more uncertain notes of restoration on the basis of some "compromise," the precise terms of which were left cloudy but surely would have included concessions to the Slave Power and a reward to Union-dissolvers, encouraging them to use disunion as a future weapon for extortionate purposes.[58]

To lose the election would be to lose all. The dead would have died uselessly. Even a successful reunion based on terms of compromise would be a permanent, fatal indictment of the Republican Party for having waded the country hip-deep in gore in the first place when an easier route to union could have been found by those who insisted throughout the war that they were the only people fitted to govern and always had been. But Republicans did not imagine that compromise could restore the Union nor a cease-fire lead to negotiations that would make out of two nations one. They remembered well the words of Sen. Louis Wigfall of Texas in 1861, when he warned that even if the North signed a blank paper and allowed seceded states to write the terms for reunion, the South would reject them. It was gone for good.[59] A pause in the fighting, then, would only assure a diseevered country, divided in two for the moment and split still further the next time one lost an election and took upon itself the right of revolution. Law itself would dissolve, with those who broke the nation's fundamental law amply rewarded for their temerity. Life or death hung on the Republicans' survival—and, quite possibly, hangings hung on it as well. An angry people might well do as some Democrats were suggesting and bring out their ropes to swing the factionists and abolitionists whose policies had cost America so much treasure and blood.[60]

In such a situation Republicans could swallow resentments far more easily and, when the conventions were over and the nominations made, launch the best fight they had in them. They could do it because they were not just fighting for office this time but for their lives, politically and perhaps personally. They were also fighting for the life of their country, which this time truly was in peril, the same peril that politicians had raised election after election until the warnings took on a threadbare consistency.

So Lincoln's escape from the perils of patronage was not just due to his deftness of touch. He owed it not to the honored fed but to the honored dead from which the party took increased devotion and to ideologues and politicians who, for the highest-minded of reasons as well as the lowest, highly resolved that government of the Republic, by the Republicans, and for the Republicans should not perish from the earth.

That may have been accomplishment enough, but it is worth noticing what patronage did not, and could not, do. Just as the spoils system really did not matter much to helping the Union win the war and in this brief, unusual moment had lost its power to harm those who played with such double-edged tools as office-broking, there were even bigger and more dramatic things that it could not do. All the spoils that New York could offer could not put William Seward back on top of politics there, and all the cunning service that Treasury agents could give to Salmon Chase could not carry him close to taking the presidential nomination from Lincoln. In fact, three months before the convention Chase broke the deafening silence at the very mention of his name as a candidate by taking himself out of the running.

There were even more dramatic things that never happened. Let dreamers imagine that handing out offices was the first step in making a new Republican Party nationwide or forming a loyal Republican south. Nothing of the kind happened. Both goals the Republicans had and both of them Lincoln shared with party organizers. The 1860 election had been a fluke in which a divided democracy made Republican success possible. The "party of moral ideas" could not count on any such miracle in 1864 or thereafter. Democrats were the majority party among white voters nationwide and knew it. Indeed, until 1896 no Republican president carried a majority of white Americans. What was to follow?

Seven score and four years ago it was nowhere near as clear as it is now that two parties, so conceived and so dedicated, could long endure. In wartime and for a generation beyond observers prophesied realignment. Take away the Republicans' chief issue, slavery, and its members would look for new political homes. Old Democrats hankered after their old allegiances when the cruel war was over. Whigs foresaw a new edifice built on a solid Clay foundation, the program of tariff protection and economic promotion that Henry Clay had designed. New parties must arise to replace the old. That seemed natural because that was how it had been in the past. The Whig Party had lasted only twenty years, and the Federalists barely any longer. Most politicians past middle age could remember when they had run for office under another banner with what now must have seemed a strange device.

If the Republican Party were to survive it must broaden its appeal in the South and among those conservatives who had hesitated in 1860, so Republicans went all out to display their Democratic converts and magnify them into a mighty force. The War Democrats lent their names and limbered up their lungs for the cause, sure enough. But did the rank and file follow? Results differed, state by state, location by location. In southern Illinois, "Egypt," as it was called, the Hebrew host made lasting conversions. Within a generation Republicans would have strongholds where once Stephen A. Douglas had been unbeatable. New, stronger Union parties grew out of Democratic factions in Oregon and California. Indeed, everywhere fresh to statehood, where partisan divisions remained relatively unformed, the war and its aftermath allowed a new political deal.[61]

But mostly the election figures show that Democrats stayed Democratic and Republicans stayed Republican. Gen. George McClellan lost badly in 1864; he might have won badly had the war not made a sharp turn for the better in the last few months before the election and without some generous help from the "soldier vote"—which, Democrats insisted, was generous to a fault, the fault being intimidation of Democratic soldiers and the creative counting of Lincoln voters. The actual numbers that Democrats won from northern states were not that far from a majority.[62] The realignment had not happened.

Nor would it happen after the war, however much patronage was applied to bring such a result. Andrew Johnson's call for a National Union Party looked to Democrats like the chance they needed to make a friendly takeover of the administration and of Republicans' labels and catch phrases; conservative Republicans saw it as a way of kicking more radical members out and making up losses elsewhere; and everyone knew that the way to the public's heart was through fifty thousand officeholders' and five hundred thousand office-seekers' stomachs. The public's hearts went untouched, the National Union Party died with scarcely a mourner to do it reverence, and quite a lot of Republican officeholders just went—some almost welcoming the chance to be casualties for the true faith.[63] When a realignment of sorts did come in the 1870s it was more of a half-shift. Instead of making a new party system, it changed the comparative share of the vote that Republicans and Democrats received without changing what the two parties stood for.[64] Fresh organizations did arise, but they were no more than "sideshow" parties, refuges for the chronic discontented and good on Election Day for no more than 1 or 2 percent of the vote unless a major party stood sponsor and paid their bills.

And what of the South? Patronage could not make a party from nothing, but it could shore up a party in dire straits, as it had the Democrats in the late 1850s. It was among the inducements that could be tendered, and it could form an organization on the grounds that might have some chance of recruiting a rank and file to turn out on election day.

The fear of that organization had been among the dreaded results that secessionists had foreseen when Republicans marched into Washington. South of the Ohio, the militants knew, were vultures, traitors, cowards, dastards, and sell-outs, silent as long as they had no financial interest in the outcome and ready to hand the slave states over to abolitionists for a share of the pottage. Not just distrust of the North but of white southerners pushed the Rhetts and Yanceys to carry the slave states out of the Union and beyond the reach of contagion. Let Republicans appoint a postmaster in every southern town and the nucleus of an antislavery party would germinate. From there, every inch that slaveholders held would mark contested ground, either from white yeomen or black slaves inspired to rise and shake off their chains by the faintest promise of federal support.[65]

At least such was the fear. The reality, as the Lincoln administration eventually proved, was nothing so dire. Republicans wanted a southern party and were willing to pay for it in offices and rewards. But the new Republican governments could not turn offices into popular majorities. They won most of their votes only by culling the electorate to get rid of as many Democrats as possible. The loyal government of Arkansas was so weak that a breath could puff it away, and its senators could not earn the respectability for Congress to admit them to seats. In Virginia, Francis Pierpont's authority stretched barely beyond Alexandria and perished out of sight of the Potomac. Without the tacit backing of federal troops it would have dissolved, and it lived on sufferance until an election could heave it out.[66] "Secession never was so intolerant, so ripe, so rampant as it is here at this time," a Virginian complained.

The picture in Missouri, Maryland, and Tennessee was little better. Unionists could win elections and ratify the Thirteenth Amendment, abolishing slavery. But it wasn't giving offices that put Republicans in charge, it was taking away votes—the disfranchisement of former Confederates and their sympathizers. Even then, they lasted barely long enough to warm their chairs. By 1870 Maryland, Tennessee, Missouri, and West Virginia were lost, not to be recovered for two generations. With plenty of patronage but no chance to purge the polls, Republicans never had a chance in Delaware, and Kentucky all but joined the Confederacy as soon as the war was over.[67]

Louisiana should have proven the heartbreaking truth most plainly. There, Republicans had three years to use their patronage before the war ended and build a party machine. With Gen. Nathaniel P. Banks to suggest the kind of constitution that a free state should have, and with the power to appoint and remove wholly in his hands, Louisiana did create a semblance of a Lincoln Union Party in and around New Orleans. But "much office-seeking, and no mean amount of venality" could never harmonize the Unionists in general.[68] The conservatives refused to be taken into camp, and the more radical Free-Staters swore no allegiance to a government that they insisted was a hoax and unconnected to the real majority of people in Louisiana.[69]

That proved the case, for Banks's government did not even represent the white people of the Pelican State. What spoils could build up, spoils could dismantle instanter. When J. Madison Wells succeeded to the vacant gover-norship, he purged the offices of Banks's followers and put in creatures of his own. "The best recommendation that an applicant for office can bring the Governor and party is that he was in the rebel army, while a Yankee brought here by the war or the result thereof, is a barbarian to be discouraged and driven from the state," a Unionist complained.[70] The voters, most of them Confederates or their apologists, were determined to wrest the state from outlanders, and in Wells they saw the best tool for doing so. That fall they elected a fiercely Democratic legislature. Within the month Wells was finding that all his power to do favors had won him precisely nothing, not even good will. The new legislature wasted no time in stripping him of his appointive powers.[71] The governor's main strength had lain in the president's support, not in his legal authority.[72] When that, too, was lost, Wells was the lamest of lame ducks, and hunting season was in full swing. His only chance, and that of the Unionists, was the same one that had given a flickering half-life to Republican parties elsewhere in the South: cut enough whites out of the vote and give the ballot to enough blacks to rig the political system their way. White conservatives stopped the plan before it started. When the remnants of the 1864 constitutional convention met, bent on mischief, the streets ran with blood.[73]

The swag-based southern strategy did not end in Lincoln's time. Money went into propping up party newspapers across the South and appointing that indispensable Democrat here or there who might bring legions of former Confederates into party ranks. All the dreams ended with rude awakenings.

Building new parties from political sweets was the kind of fantasy fit only for fooling politicians. Gingerbread houses are not meant to last.

We should not take this shabby story too seriously. Instead of arguing that the good cause was shot through with selfishness, it might be that in this case even selfishness and ambition worked to ends higher than personal gain and that from private vices came the greatest of public benefits. The Civil War was no scoundrel time, and for that give credit to the confines into which the spoils system worked. Out of the conflict came no dictator, no Caesar, the way Democrats had feared, and for that the rules about who had a say in appointing whom should get the credit. The president should be given a pass for permitting plunder along the Potomac.

In the end, after all, there was not much else he could have done. Practical rather than theoretical in all other things and willing to have God on his side but aware that he must have Kentucky, he took on fights he could win. The fight to save the Union: that was possible. The fight to drive greed and self-interest out of a politics powered by both was as mad as making a southern Republican Party out of customshouse clerks and post office poll workers. Lincoln may never have thought about doing so at all. Detest the office-seekers' short-sightedness though he might, he never seemed to have considered trying to change the system he had used so earnestly on his own way up the political ladder. If he had, he very likely would have put off making changes until another time. For well he knew—as well we know—that it is a far easier thing to strike the mystic chords of memory than to strike off the fetters of favoritism in public life.

4. "Seeking a Cause of Difficulty with the Government"

Reconsidering Freedom of Speech and Judicial Conflict under Lincoln

MARK E. NEELY JR.

Over the years, historians have found considerable drama in the often tense relationship between Abraham Lincoln and the U.S. Congress during the Civil War. The president's relations with the other branch of government, the judiciary, have generally been characterized by describing a brief and early skirmish on which the curtain closed quickly. In fact, the president's relations with Congress were not as bad as once thought, for the legislative branch was dominated by fellow Republicans and when the chips were down, as elections approached, the party closed ranks. Moreover, in wartime the American Constitution tips heavily toward the executive branch, and Lincoln, far from being at a disadvantage with Congress, actually held the upper hand in war matters.

His relationship with the judicial branch was more problematic and deserves more attention than it has received. Years of Democratic political dominance had left the Supreme Court and many other courts in the hands of Democratic judges who had tenure in office. The rhythm of the election calendar did not particularly affect the relations between executive and judiciary. Even in the case of the well-known skirmish between the president and the chief justice of the Supreme Court of the United States, which historians have recognized for its dramatic potential, the drama has been underestimated.

* * *

In the case of *Ex parte Merryman*, the political future of the United States was at stake. Such an assertion may seem to defy the logic of the American

Constitution. After all, Alexander Hamilton had assured Americans in *The Federalist* number 78 that the judiciary would be "the least dangerous [department] to the political rights of the Constitution." It "can take no active resolution whatever," Hamilton asserted. "It may truly be said to have neither FORCE nor WILL but merely judgment."[1]

By the time Chief Justice Roger B. Taney was leading the Supreme Court onto a collision course with the Republican administration of Abraham Lincoln, Hamilton's view of the judicial branch did not really fit the role of the judiciary in American politics. The aged chief justice, who had led the court for well over two decades when Lincoln came to power, may have looked fragile, but he had a forceful and willful attitude toward the sectional crisis, and his political sympathies lay decidedly on the south side of the Potomac.[2] Taney was a dangerous man.

During the Civil War, Taney attempted to play a role analogous to that John Marshall had played a half-century earlier in establishing an ever-larger role in American politics for the judiciary as a way to thwart major reversal in the U.S. political landscape. Marshall's motivation had been substantially political and so was Taney's.

After the election of 1860, secession, and the firing on Fort Sumter, the Supreme Court under Taney was in a position like that of the Court under Marshall after the election of Thomas Jefferson in 1800. Marshall's Federalist Party, terribly split by the factional feud between its great leaders John Adams and Alexander Hamilton, now faced Jeffersonian Republican control of the Congress and the presidency. Only the little-tested federal judiciary, stacked with Federalist appointees from the previous administrations of John Adams and George Washington and insulated from political removal by life tenure, stood in the path of an overwhelming Republican tide. Marshall discovered or invigorated powers of review that let the judiciary stand athwart that seemingly inexorable political reversal of Federalist dominance.

Both the Jeffersonian Republican Party and that of Lincoln appeared to their partisan enemies to be animated by a fanaticism that threatened the foundations of the Republic. The opposition felt justified in exploiting all the constitutional powers available to obstruct them. Taney attempted the same feat Marshall had but failed either to reverse the political tide or to enhance the role of the judicial branch. Of course, he was, thanks to Marshall, already armed with judicial review. In the Dred Scott decision four years earlier, Taney had, for the first time in generations, asserted the Court's power to overturn a major piece of congressional legislation. But war would not wait on the appeals process. What he needed now was a way to assert the considerable powers of the judiciary without waiting. After all, the Dred Scott case had been eleven years in the making, and no one thought the Civil War would last anything like that long.

Taney needed original jurisdiction, the one power the otherwise *Supreme Court* did not possess in most cases. Once he gained center stage, he could discover or invigorate the idea of civil liberty with respect to executive power in wartime, but how could the Supreme Court seize the limelight? Taney discovered that he could assert judicial power rather than wait passively for cases to come to him on appeal because war offered a rare opportunity for Supreme Court justices to exercise original jurisdiction. Under section 14 of the Judiciary Act of 1789, Supreme Court justices enjoyed original jurisdiction in habeas corpus applications brought by federal prisoners. War would produce an abundance of federal prisoners, a novelty in the early nineteenth century, and thus an abundance of habeas corpus appeals to all the higher judiciary. In a great political gamble, the chief justice of the Supreme Court seized that power as soon as the circumstance of civil war in Maryland, his home state, permitted.

To take this view of the Merryman case imputes considerable partisan drive to a man who hid it, if he possessed it, very skillfully, but, in the absence of documentary evidence on Taney's motives, it is plausible. Such an interpretation also imputes considerable sectionalism to a Marylander who had manumitted his own slaves long ago. But the intervening Dred Scott decision itself, as the great constitutional historian Don E. Fehrenbacher has shown, makes that identification with the South obvious.[3]

Taney was surely partisan enough to observe with alarm the fortunes of his party. The Democrats, as the Civil War began, were hopelessly split, and after war broke out their strongest leader, in the absence of the many able Southerners who were departing the Union, was Stephen A. Douglas of Illinois. The Southern-sympathizing Taney would attempt to offer alternative leadership to Douglas's stout Unionism, and with the death of Douglas in June he would be in effect grasping at leadership of the whole Democratic cause.

As always, the best evidence lies in Taney's printed judicial opinions, in this case, *Ex parte Merryman*. John Merryman, from whom the case took its name, was a Marylander. His state sat on the route from the North that troops had to take to protect the nation's capital. In the panicky early days of the Civil War, Washington seemed dangerously exposed to capture by Southern troops. People in Baltimore rioted against the passage of Northern troops through the city to the rescue of the capital. Merryman, as an officer in a local military organization who had openly expressed secession sentiments, naturally drew the attention of Union soldiers whose duty it was to protect the nation's capital. He was arrested in his own house, in Cockeysville, north of Baltimore, at two in the morning of May 25, 1861. The president had suspended the writ of habeas corpus in the area around Washington already, but on the next day a lawyer representing Merryman petitioned Roger B. Taney for a writ of habeas corpus, which would require the soldiers to produce Merryman in court and explain to the judge under what charge and authority they held the prisoner. By law, of course, they had none, and they were not about to produce him in court.[4]

Gen. George Cadwalader held the prisoner at Fort McHenry in Baltimore but was uncertain of the cause of the arrest, which was made by officers beyond his area of command. Nevertheless, Cadwalader was served with the writ of habeas corpus to appear in court on Monday the 27. He declined to produce the prisoner but sent a colonel with a written explanation of his role in the case. After dealing in the courtroom on May 28 with the army's refusal to produce the prisoner, Taney drafted his decision, which came from the "Chief Justice of the Supreme Court of the United States, at Chambers," that is, not from a regular term of the whole Court. He aimed the written opinion at the president of the United States and at the press.[5]

Confusion persists about the nature of the Merryman decision. Was it a circuit court ruling or a Supreme Court ruling? Obviously, that is a matter of more than technical interest. The problem lies in the place where historians read the decision today, in the federal court reports as 17 *Fed. Cas.* No. 9487 (1861) 144–53 and not in the Supreme Court reports. In other words, the problem inheres in the fact that Taney held the hearing not in the Supreme Court in Washington but in the federal circuit court in Baltimore.[6]

But the decision was not merely a federal circuit court ruling. Taney made explicit in *Ex parte Merryman* itself that the petition for a writ of habeas corpus had first been presented to him in Washington, D.C., and that his jurisdiction in the matter stemmed from the power each justice of the Supreme Court possessed to grant writs of habeas corpus for federal prisoners. Taney heard the case in the Baltimore courtroom only as a convenience to the army general who was holding the prisoner so that he would not have to leave his military post in Maryland to produce the prisoner Merryman in the District of Columbia.[7] Taney thus brilliantly anticipated a future defense of the suspensions of the writ of habeas corpus, that generals on the march or preparing for battle could, if the writ of habeas corpus were not suspended, be halted in their tracks and required to travel miles and miles to appear before a judge and explain why they held a person against his will in the army or in the stockade.

In fact, the Merryman opinion, as a political document, has been considerably underestimated. And it is as a political document that it needs to be interpreted. Like the Dred Scott decision in Fehrenbacher's eyes, this opinion too could be read the same way we read any stump speech from the middle of the nineteenth century.[8] Taney crafted the Merryman opinion carefully. It contains more than citations and technical legal language. He apparently saw to its publication in pamphlet form later. Taney did not write or read the opinion in the courtroom. It was not aimed at the defendant in the hearing or the people in the courtroom. It was written for the president to see—and for the American people to read. After writing the body of the habeas corpus opinion in the Merryman case, Taney added a brilliant flourish that preserved the crucial passive image of the judiciary. The chief justice, when the general holding the prisoner refused to produce him in court, ostentatiously bowed to "a force too strong for me to overcome."[9] While flexing the muscle of the judicial branch, Taney posed as a weakling.

The power of the decision lay not in the possibility of ordering some federal marshal to ride into an army camp and retrieve a military prisoner. It lay in what Taney did with the decision afterward. First, he had the court clerk send a copy to the president. Then he saw to its publication and dissemination. It is not clear why the case was not reported in the U.S. Supreme Court reports. The court reporter at the time of the Merryman decision, Benjamin Howard, was sitting at the clerk's desk in the Baltimore courtroom when Taney confronted the army colonel bringing word of General Cadwalader's defiance.[10] And earlier volumes of the reports had included material other than decisions of the whole court and the attendant papers.[11] Howard would resign his reporting position in September, before the relevant volume of Supreme Court reports came out, to run as the gubernatorial candidate of a peace party in Maryland.[12] A local newspaper, announcing his replacement later stated that Howard had resigned "on account of his secessionist proclivities."[13] His replacement, Jeremiah Black, was, like Howard and Taney, a fiercely loyal Democrat, but he was famous for having backed the cause of the Union while the Buchanan administration appeared to be truckling before Southern pressure; Black had no "secessionist proclivities."[14] Whatever the reason, *Ex parte Merryman* never appeared in the published Supreme Court reports.

The official publication of legal opinions and decisions was not a viable forum for a political movement, anyway. It was too slow and technical. Taney had to see the opinion distributed in the press and as a political pamphlet.[15]

As it turned out, Taney's gamble failed. The Democratic Party in the North at the beginning of the Civil War was too weak to force the Republican administration to do anything. Taney did not have the whole court behind him or any way of getting it behind his decision any time soon. Taney did not have the whole Democratic Party behind him either. Although Stephen A. Douglas's death was announced in the newspapers at the same time that Taney's decision was first printed in them, the example of Douglas's loyal opposition was too fresh and strong to be overcome. Taney blazed the trail of discovery of civil liberties by the Democratic Party, but as yet the Democrats' throbbing nationalism tended to ignore Republican transgressions against such liberties. The image of the powerless judiciary persisted, however, and may have been Taney's only lasting legacy from the dark period of his chief justiceship during the Civil War.

* * *

The drama of conflict between the national executive power and the judges did not end there, although in some accounts of the constitutional and political history of the war it seems to. Stanley I. Kutler's *Judicial Power and Reconstruction Politics* depicted the Civil War as a time of surprising partisan agreement on the secure role of the Supreme Court and the federal courts in the American system.[16] In the broader-ranging constitutional and legal history of the period written by Harold M. Hyman, *A More Perfect Union: The Impact of the Civil War and Reconstruction on the Constitution,* a similar consensus view prevails. In a typical passage, this one concluding his discussion of the Habeas Corpus Act of 1863, Hyman states, "No more Taney-Lincoln confrontations occurred. The increased national court jurisdiction provided by Congress prevented constitutional crises. Ordinary court processes and familiar political procedures, including elections, avoided clashes between nation and state. The enlargement of national court jurisdiction was more than a duration-only step. It was the beginning of an end to some of federalism's twilight zones which had helped to bring on the Civil War."[17]

It is surprising to see how much these important books on the Constitution during the war focus on legislative history for attitudes toward courts and Constitution rather than on judicial behavior itself in courtrooms and judicial chambers across the country.

The judiciary during the Civil War remains one of the very few neglected subjects for research on the era, and this chapter is an attempt to suggest the promising nature of such research and its potential for causing historians to revise their views of Lincoln and civil liberties. In what follows, I will focus on a single case involving freedom of speech, the military power, and the Lincoln administration. The point is that more such dramas of confrontation and near-conflict can surely be found. The case under examination here stemmed from the arrest in 1863 of a Democratic newspaper editor named Albert D. Boileau by military authorities in Philadelphia. What is particularly interesting about the incident is the view it provides of the power of courts of all sorts in the North during the Civil War to exert will and force against the army and the administration behind it. To understand the case will require going back in time to the formation of the Republic to recapture the history of a little-known legal institution, the charge to the grand jury.

* * *

The charge to the grand jury, a speech by a judge explaining to grand jurors their duties, had been widely used by Federalists on the federal bench in the early days after the adoption of the Constitution. Modern constitutional historians generously credit it as an "educational" device employed by judicial "schoolmasters" for informing the people about the new form of government under the Constitution drafted in Philadelphia in 1787.[18] But there could be too much of a good thing, and when Federalist judges began using the charge to the grand jury after the election of Thomas Jefferson as president to denounce the new administration, Republicans mounted a crusade to end such usage.[19] The Jeffersonians hauled out the heaviest artillery in the constitutional arsenal to attack it: impeachment.

They focused on Samuel Chase of Maryland, a justice on the Supreme Court. In 1803 he gave a charge to a grand jury in Baltimore that constituted an anti-Republican stump speech, and a virulent one at that. Chase was reeling from recent Republican attacks on the Federalist judiciary now that the Republicans so thoroughly controlled Congress and the presidency, and in his rambling charge he criticized the Republican assault on the judicial branch at both the state and national level. He also denounced the advent of universal manhood suffrage in the state of Maryland, where the circuit court was located. He ended his judicial harangue by saying, "The change of the state constitution by allowing universal suffrage, will in my opinion certainly and rapidly destroy all protection to property, and all security to personal liberty; and our Republican constitution will sink into a *mobocracy*, the worst of all possible governments."[20] In 1804 the House of Representatives impeached Chase on eight articles. The first six accusations were based on his actions in cases stemming from the infamous Sedition Act, but the seventh and eighth dealt with the justice's charges to grand juries.

In the seventh article of impeachment, the House of Representatives alleged that Chase, while on circuit in Delaware, had "stooped to the level of an informer" by insisting that a grand jury, which had declared that it had no presentments to make, examine the case of a newspaper printer in the state who published seditious articles. Chase had ordered the district attorney to obtain a run of the papers as evidence for the jury to examine.[21] The members of Congress disagreed on the facts alleged in this impeachment article, and it failed miserably in the final Senate vote on the articles.[22] Controversy over the role of a judge in himself volunteering such information to a grand jury would figure in an important way in the judicial proceedings following the arrest of Albert Boileau during the Civil War.

The eighth article singled out, as essentially seditious, ironically, Chase's charge to the Baltimore grand jury. He had, the impeachment managers alleged, in "an intemperate and inflammatory political harangue" attempted to "excite the fears and resentment . . . of the good people of Maryland against their State government . . . [and] against the Government of the United States."[23] The Senate failed to convict Chase on any of the articles of impeachment, but the standard text in American constitutional history maintains that "the prosecution had its strongest case" on the eighth article, the one concerning the charge to the grand jury in Baltimore.[24] Indeed, the vote that came closest to conviction came on that eighth article.

The opinion seems to be general that the political charge to the grand jury died out as a practice afterward. That might be true in the case of the Supreme Court justices on circuit, although there is some evidence from the Civil War to the contrary, but it is untrue in the case of charges to the grand jury made by the judiciary of the states.[25] There, especially in the South, the practice of the political charge persisted. It was revived and on the upswing in the Civil War era.

* * *

Beginning with the intensification of the sectional crisis provoked by the rise of the Republican Party in the middle of the 1850s, politically ardent judges employed the charge to the grand jury as an aggressive weapon. This growing assertion of judicial will and force in the late 1850s and in the decade of the 1860s has gone unnoticed by political historians, but it paralleled, at the level of state and lower courts, the anti-Republican and pro-slavery activism of the Supreme Court under Roger B. Taney.[26] As was the case with all other political techniques, partisans responded in kind, and there are spectacular examples of political charges made by Republican judges in the period as well.[27]

To judges at the time, the charge to the grand jury stood as a judicial tradition handed down from ancient British practice and seamlessly carried over into the life of the Republic. As historian Ralph Lerner describes it, "The prevailing practice was for a judge to summarize for a newly empaneled grand jury the statutes and, in the state courts, the common law relevant to the performance of their duty."[28] Grand juries in those days offered more than indictments (on evidence presented by a district attorney) and presentments (recommendations for prosecution based on their own knowledge).[29] They also surveyed the general condition of the public institutions of the jurisdiction, the poor house, roads, bridges, and public buildings, and commented on public nuisances and threats to community morality. As one observer who knew the work of Pennsylvania grand juries put it in 1800,

> A kind of censorial authority is sometimes exercised by the grand jury. Viewing themselves not as the representatives, but as a respectable collection, of the people of the county, they consider it proper to express, in a public manner, their united sentiments of public inconveniences, improvements, or other transactions, measures, or things, of a general nature, and affecting the welfare of the county, or on which it is proper for their voice to be known; express praise or blame, according to their nature or tendency; and suggest or recommend the prosecution of public benefits, and redress of public gr[ie]vances. In this, they act not in their official capacity nor is the exercise of this authority founded on any law. This authority is founded only on use, and a presumed public convenience; and, when exercised discreetly it may be attended with good effects.[30]

In other words, they voiced political concerns. Perhaps because of that latitude taken by grand jurors, the judges in their charges to grand juries often deviated considerably from the narrowly judicial to the generally political as well. Grand jury charges became in some instances stump speeches delivered by judges and printed in the party newspapers.[31]

The acrimonious politics of the 1850s and 1860s reinvigorated the institution. The most famous antebellum example came in Bleeding Kansas. A federal judge played a crucial role, in fact, in inciting the "Sack of Lawrence" in 1856. Samuel Lecompte, the chief justice of the supreme court of Kansas Territory, charged the grand jury in Lecompton to take action against the Free State government located in Lawrence. Posses formed in Lecompton subsequently traveled to Lawrence and after arresting two people charged by the grand jury after Lecompte's speech, engaged in mob actions that resulted in the destruction of the newspaper office and hotel and in the robbery and vandalizing of the town's shops.[32]

Civil War politics in the North were nearly as acrimonious as those in Bleeding Kansas before the war, and the temptation to assert the force and will of the judiciary was great. In Philadelphia in 1863 an irate Democratic judge succumbed. James R. Ludlow, judge of the Quarter Sessions Court in Philadelphia, learned on the last day of the court session of the arrest by military authorities of Albert D. Boileau, editor of the Philadelphia *Evening Journal* and a longtime active Democrat. The authorities had arrested the editor around midnight and rushed him out of Philadelphia to Fort McHenry, which had once held John Merryman, also a victim of arrest after midnight.[33] Ludlow seized upon his power to charge the grand jury as a way to bring about the arrest of the military officials who had arrested Boileau. He charged the grand jury to investigate the event and sent the district attorney to fetch the persons who he had heard caused the arrest in Philadelphia—officers in the Union Army. "Gentlemen," Ludlow said, "I have alone taken the responsibility of addressing you to-day."[34]

Judge Ludlow said that Philadelphians had stood by long enough while people were abducted from the city. In fact, Ludlow delivered something approaching a stump speech although it lacked the partisan markers customary on the stump and was a good deal more restrained than Samuel Chase's. He pointed out that the courts of the state and nation were open, "magistrates abound at every corner of the streets, . . . known to be loyal men . . . peace reigns in this county, and no impending danger destroys the authority of law. . . . Did the people of this Commonwealth," he asked rhetorically, "when they entered into the Union ever agree to devolve upon either the President of the United States, Congress, or the Judiciary, or all three combined, the power to suspend the privilege of the writ of habeas corpus in a State or district when the 'public safety did not require it?'" He assailed the continuing "arbitrary arrests" in the county but did not cite any precedent or quote any specific law in the nine paragraphs of his charge. He did, however, call on the grand jurors "to sustain a right as clear as the noonday sun, as vital as life-giving breath, without the existence of which the Government itself is a stupendous deception."[35] The charge quickly appeared in Philadelphia newspapers.

Ludlow's Court of Quarter Sessions was the criminal court of Philadelphia County, in which the city was contained. It was not his bench alone but was served by three judges. Except in murder cases, they presided individually over the court, apparently alternating from session to session. At this period in Pennsylvania history the judges were elected for ten-year terms. In addition to Ludlow, Oswald Thompson and Joseph Allison sat on the bench. Ludlow, elected in 1857, was the only Democrat. Allison and Thompson had been reelected in 1861.[36]

Individual Supreme Court justices enjoyed the power to hear habeas corpus pleas for federal prisoners, but even in the case of the highest court in the land the authoritative quality of an opinion grew with the number of justices involved.[37] *Ex parte Merryman* would have been political dynamite had it been a decision of the whole Court rather than a decision of one justice in chambers. In the case of a court of oyer and terminer—a criminal court, in other words—in Philadelphia, like the Quarter Sessions court, authority was surely increased by convening all three of its judges, which could apparently be done in important cases. At least two had to be present in homicide cases, as it was, and Judges Ludlow and Allison had the previous week presided over a murder case.[38] Surely it would have been prudent and rational to convene the court en banc for a case that might bring this petty jurisdiction into conflict with the president of the United States and the U.S. Army in wartime. But Judge Ludlow was a Democrat and had no desire to call into consultation his Republican colleague, Judge Allison.

The situation Judge Ludlow faced was this. Boileau's Philadelphia *Evening Journal,* in its issue of January 20, 1863, compared Abraham Lincoln's most recent annual message to Congress with Jefferson Davis's and concluded that Davis had more "intellectual capacity." The *Evening Journal* added that Davis's recent speeches contained the truth about the war. Gen. Robert Schenck, a Republican politician-turned-general who had been wounded at the Second Battle of Manassas and subsequently given a desk job as commander of the Middle Department with headquarters at Baltimore, took a stern view of criticism of the government in war.[39] He gave the order on January 24 to arrest Boileau for the content of the newspaper's editorial comparing Davis and Lincoln "and for the publication of other articles of like dangerous character tending to the support and encouragement of Rebellion." It fell to Gen. William Montgomery to arrest the editor. Montgomery, in turn, apparently got the Philadelphia provost marshal to bring Boileau in.[40]

At Judge Ludlow's request to suspend all other business before them, the dutiful grand jurors listened to testimony from General Montgomery, from the provost marshal, and from various people employed at the newspaper.

The grand jurors offered a circumspect presentment.[41] They professed their desire to suppress the rebellion while still enforcing all the laws. They identified the men who had arrested Boileau, and they reprinted most of the controversial editorial that had provoked Schenck. The judge rushed the presentment to the district attorney, for not only was the term of the court ending that Saturday evening but the new term that would open the next Monday would be called to order under the gavel of the Republican, Judge Allison.

Nothing came of the case constitutionally because friends of Boileau traveled to Maryland, where he was imprisoned, and to Washington, where there were higher administration authorities to appeal to. The authorities intervened, and Boileau was persuaded to make an apology and promise never to "write, print, or publish any articles having such dangerous character" again.[42] In exchange, Union authorities released him from military prison. Boileau's humiliating statement was widely published in the press.

But as was the case in other instances—and perhaps in instances as yet undiscovered—the constitutional controversy was a near miss and had the potential for serious conflict between the judiciary and the executive. The prospect of the Philadelphia district attorney prosecuting the local provost marshal or a general of the army in the tense summer of 1863, when Pennsylvania was invaded by Robert E. Lee's army, held potential for more than judicial drama. In any event, politically, the case was not over yet.

Judge Allison saw to that. His charge to the grand jury was a response to Judge Ludlow's. If it was not exactly a stump speech itself and relied more on legal precedent, it did put that precedent to somewhat surprising use. Allison did his research and cited a decision limiting the scope of grand jury action, *In the Matter of the Communication of the Grand Jury in the Case of Lloyd and Carpenter,* a Pennsylvania case from 1845 that was reported in a short-lived legal periodical published in the state. In the Lloyd and Carpenter case, when grand jurors attempted to investigate fraud in the Philadelphia Board of Health, Judge Edward King refused to call witnesses or force the board to produce its books. The Lloyd and Carpenter decision is now regarded as part of a general movement toward limitation of grand jury power, but Allison read it ultimately as a limitation on the power of the judge.[43] If grand jurors could not act on information supplied by anyone outside their group, *including the judge,* then the judge could not bring about the grand jury's action on any individual case.

Allison was correct in characterizing the Lloyd and Carpenter decision as one that illustrated the "extraordinary" nature of grand jury proceedings to bring about the punishment of crimes. Later citations of the Lloyd and Carpenter precedent likewise employed it to reveal the differences between "ordinary" procedures in criminal cases and extraordinary ones called for by "special circumstances."[44] The rest was special to Allison's reading. It was quite all right, he pointed out, for the presiding judge to "call the attention of grand juries to and direct investigation of matters of general public import, which from their nature and operation in the entire community, justify such intervention. The action of courts rather bears on things than persons, the object being the suppression of general and public evils."[45] In other words, custom had made it acceptable that the judge in his charge take notice of the conditions of public institutions in the jurisdiction as grand juries had long been doing. Individual criminal activity, however, was a carefully defined matter.

The Lloyd and Carpenter decision, according to Allison, made it clear that a grand jury presentment was an extraordinary mode of bringing about process for crime and could not be aided by the court itself. Allison said that grand jury presentment "must be founded exclusively upon *their own knowledge or observations; they cannot act on information communicated by any one* outside of their own body, nor can they be aided in their investigation against individual offenders, whom they may desire to present for indictment by the process of the Court."[46]

Judge Allison's objections to Ludlow's action hinged on two critical points, one essentially legal and the other essentially political. The legal point was devastating. Judge Ludlow's procedure "would constitute a power of a most fearful and despotic nature . . . for the same officer who procures the indict-ment of an individual defendant for a specific offense, would have the power to try and sentence him when brought into Court *by his direct agency.*"[47] In other words, he should not serve as both prosecutor and judge. Ludlow, it might be said, had run afoul of Samuel Chase's problem in the seventh article of impeachment. Ludlow had, to borrow the language of that article, "stooped to the level of an informer."

Allison's political point was that Ludlow's charge was "injudicious, for however well intended, the consequence of a judge, of his own motion, upon mere information obtained in no legal way, for here was no complaint under oath, with unnecessary and unusual haste, making use of his official posi-tion to institute a prosecution strictly personal and private in its nature, is to render the whole proceeding liable to misconstruction; to place this Court in a false position before the country, as anxious for, and of its own motion, seeking a cause of difficulty with the Government."[48] In other words, Allison saw in it the aggressive assertion of judicial power by a Democratic judge politically at odds with the Republican administration in Washington.

* * *

Taken together, the Boileau arrest and the judicial and political reaction to it, reveal the great potential for conflict between executive and judiciary in the Civil War. Historians need to recall that the judiciary could be aggressive, too. But the Boileau arrest can hardly be dismissed with an examination of jurisdictional problems and the potential for conflict in the branches of the government. It was also an important and sensational instance of the restric-tion of press freedom by the Lincoln administration. Surely, Judge Ludlow had in mind the protection of press freedom in his aggressive maneuver-ing on Boileau's behalf. Does the case, whatever the judicial irregularity of Ludlow's methods, somehow stand properly as a reminder of attempts of the opposition Democrats in the Civil War to keep alive the ideal of freedom of the press in the midst even of civil war?

I examined twelve Pennsylvania newspapers as well as the influential press in New York City—the *World, Times, Tribune, Herald,* and *Evening Post*—for reactions to the Boileau arrest and to subsequent judicial maneuvers.[49] The reaction of the press is a reminder that freedom of the press still eluded the Civil War generation, at least in wartime. Newspapers of the other party got what they deserved.

The party press never broke ranks. Republican newspapers tended to applaud Boileau's arrest. The Harrisburg *Telegraph* expressed surprise that he had not been arrested earlier and his *Evening Journal* long since suppressed because Boileau was "a traitor" and his newspaper had repeatedly expressed sympathy for treason.[50] The Washington (Pennsylvania) *Reporter and Tribune,* also Republican, wrote at some length on the Boileau case, comparing the attitudes of the Pennsylvania legislature of Revolutionary days and the attitude of 1863. Democrats in the state legislature mounted a campaign to get the Republican governor to go to Washington to recover the prisoner and return him to the state. The *Reporter* regarded those in the state legislature seeking Boileau's release—all Democrats—as "ready champions of the right of rebel sympathizers to pursue their vocation without disturbance or restraint." In the better days of the Revolution, the Continental Congress has instructed Pennsylvania to act against British sympathizers. After Boileau published his apology they characterized him as "a professed promoter of sedition" and pointed out that in the finer days of the Republic "freedom of speech was not allowed to become the shield of disloyal sympathies and seditious practices."[51]

The Harrisburg *Telegraph*'s Democratic rival, the Harrisburg *Patriot and Union,* ridiculed Republican criticism "of a learned law judge" such as Ludlow. The editors in their protests of the arrest placed roughly equal weight on "the freedom of the citizen" and on the fact that the "sovereignty of Pennsylvania has been violated."[52] They maintained that their course in protesting would have been the same had the person arrested been the hated Pennsylvania Republican Simon Cameron or even their rival, the despised editor of the Harrisburg *Telegraph.*[53]

The York *Gazette,* another Democratic newspaper, criticized the arrest on the grounds of "outrage to the rights of the citizen and the insult to the sovereignty of Pennsylvania." In the end, they despaired that so much Democratic effort had gone into defending a man who proved, by his abject apology to General Schenck, too craven to be worth the effort.[54] By contrast, the extremist peace Democratic newspaper in Centre County, Pennsylvania, the *Democratic Watchman* of Bellefonte, put by far the greatest stress on state rights: "[I]f State lines, State laws and State Rights are to be entirely crushed out, then may we well exclaim GOD SAVE THE COMMONWEALTH!"[55]

The Democratic press went untested on the question of what sort of protest it would mount if a Republican newspaper were interfered with, of course, so it was easy to say, as the Harrisburg *Patriot and Union* had, that they would defend the Republican press if the shoe were on the other foot. In fact, however, the adversarial character of the press of the era, unprofessionalized and largely incapable of viewing the interests of their industry apart from their partisan antagonism to newspapers of the other political party, meant that newspapers in the nineteenth century rarely united across partisan lines to defend the interests of the press in general. Perhaps more to the point, it also meant that the press advocated muzzling the press—as long as it was the press of the opposite party. Such was the position of the Republican press in Pennsylvania on the Boileau case, as exemplified in the Harrisburg *Telegraph* and the Washington *Reporter and Tribune*.[56]

The more independent newspapers could make fairly evenhanded observations, but they were not based on a resounding belief in the sanctity of freedom of speech. The moderate *Public Ledger,* for example, resignedly accepted Allison's decision not to send the district attorney after the officers who had, perhaps wrongfully, arrested the newspaper editor Boileau. "Judge Allison," the editors observed icily, "has the advantage of occupying the bench; therefore his law must be the ruling law till a full bench decides otherwise."[57] Before Judge Allison weighed in on the case, however, the editors of the *Public Ledger* had derived a rather different lesson from the arrest of Boileau and its aftermath. They could "see no public necessity for arrests impressed with such an arbitrary character" but were "not disposed . . . to make a factious opposition to it."[58]

The Democrats of 1863 were sufficiently lacking in intellectual and political traditions of freedom to invoke that they grasped at alien sources. Thus the New York *World,* the Democratic newspaper on which lesser Democratic sheets relied for systematic commentary on the Boileau case, found itself relying for a defense of free speech on Jeremy Bentham and British utilitarianism—an intellectual tradition that never gained much foothold in the nineteenth-century United States: "The relations of free discussion to the commonwealth have never been stated with more force than by that great and intrepid thinker, Jeremy Bentham, who has contributed more than any other writer to the enlightened spirit of reform which distinguished the present century. 'Precipitate censure,' he says, 'cast on a political institution [or measure] does but recoil on the head of him who casts it. From such an attack it is not the institution itself, if well grounded, that can suffer.'"[59]

In the end, all Democratic protests of the Boileau case during the Civil War took some version of state rights into account despite the obvious dangers of sounding as though they had embraced the seditious doctrines of Southern secessionists.

The fact of the matter is that the Democrats had too often in the sectional controversy leading up to the war given up on freedom of speech and the press. They had made many determined attempts to silence abolitionism. Even in the midst of the Civil War—less than three weeks, in fact, before the Boileau arrest—Samuel Sullivan Cox, an important Democratic leader from Ohio and a member of Congress, delivered a major address in New York City that embraced a limited view of freedom of the press. "Puritanism in Politics," as the famous speech was titled, criticized the legacy of restrictive intolerance bequeathed the nation from its New England heritage. But so intent was Cox on denouncing the abolitionist legacy of New England that he found himself also condoning attempts in the past to restrict the freedom of expression of antislavery advocates. He excused the notorious anti-abolition riots of the 1830s by saying, "The riots . . . were the instinctive out-gushings of the Union-loving masses, fearing a speech too free and a cause too reckless [to] the stability of the Government."[60]

During the Civil War, Republicans and Democrats alike thought speech could be "too free" and "reckless to the stability of the Government." Systematic explanations of protections for free expression made few advances. The Pittsburgh *Post,* a Democratic newspaper, typified the level of critical thought attained during the war in developing or discovering civil liberties. The *Post* did reprint the Bill of Rights in its pages shortly after the Boileau arrest, but it reprinted all ten amendments of the Constitution and did not focus especially on the first. It ridiculed defenses of the administration's arrest of Boileau on the grounds of military necessity in wartime, relying on the New York *World* for extended argument on that point. For its part, the *Post* spent most of its editorial effort on allegations that John Forney, the Republican editor of the Philadelphia *Press* and frequent target of Boileau editorials, must have instigated the arrest of Boileau, as though the whole affair was, as one *Post* editorial on the subject was entitled, an instance of "Malicious Mischief."[61]

For their part, Republican editors did not criticize the administration for the arrest. An exception was the New York *Tribune,* but the justification Horace Greeley's famous newspaper took was by no means rooted in the idea that the words of the press could not libel the government. In fact, the *Tribune* asserted the opposite view: "We do not approve of the manner of Mr. Boileau's arrest. We think he should have been expressly charged with treason, and thereupon arraigned for trial sitting in Philadelphia. If a civil tribunal is blocked by the disloyalty of Copperhead jurors, proclaim martial law, and try by drumhead court martial."[62]

It is difficult, of course, to know whether to take this position seriously or see the *Tribune*'s reaction like that of the Pittsburgh *Post* as incapable of dealing with the issue of freedom of the press as a momentous one reaching beyond the "mischiefs" of partisan editors accustomed to operating in a remorselessly adversarial partisan political system.

The Republican New York *Times* offered no comfort to the "Rebel Sympathizer" Boileau.[63] The independent New York *Herald* accused Greeley of "howling on and encouraging these proceedings."[64] But in keeping with the *Herald*'s customary perverse and sensationalist approach to political issues, it largely ignored the law of the matter. Instead, it pointed out that, practically speaking, such arrests were "absurd and mischievous blunders" that brought readers to newspapers that would otherwise have been left in unread obscurity. Moreover, the *Herald,* without agreeing with either party on the issue, did agree to trivialize the argument and allege that the War Department and General Schenck had been "humbugged" by John Forney into eliminating a competing newspaper. In the *Herald*'s universe there were few high matters of political philosophy, and most of American politics was reduced to venal motives and gullibility.[65] Such proved often to be the level of press criticism, debate, and discourse in the middle of the nineteenth century.

∗ ∗ ∗

Because the judiciary in Philadelphia led the Democratic attack on the Boileau arrest, the finer procedural issues received a level of careful and sophisticated treatment that was not paralleled by the discussion of perhaps larger constitutional issues of freedom of the press. These procedural arguments served, above all else, to point up the most important point illustrated by the Boileau case. The activism of the mid-century judiciary reveals itself in sharp and contentious terms. The most acute treatment of the legal issues involved in using the charge to the grand jury as a means of defending press freedom came from the Republican Judge Allison, but truth to tell, he might be accused of the same activism.

In the first place, Allison was singlehandedly reversing the legal action of a judge simply by virtue of presiding in the court on Monday that had been presided over by a judge of different opinion on Saturday.[66] Whatever he thought of Ludlow's opinion, Allison might have taken the dignity of the bench into consideration before acting. He was also repudiating the work of a grand jury. Undaunted, he ordered that the finding of the previous grand jury be ignored and that the district attorney not go forward with indictments based on it. Second, even his long and legally sophisticated refutation of Ludlow's celebrated charge to the grand jury—"Judge Ludlow's Decree," as the enthusiastic Pittsburgh *Post* described it—contained its own occasionally emotional appeals to political passions of the day, more of them than Ludlow's charge had done. Allison referred, for example, to "the spirit of malignant and treasonable faction which lives among us."[67] Although the press failed to comment on the point, Allison's procedure was as politically opportunistic as Ludlow's. When he ordered that no indictment go forth from the district attorney despite the previous grand jury's finding, he offered the qualification "without the majority of the Court's direction."[68] He did not himself call the court together en banc. Both Judge Ludlow and Judge Allison made calculated political maneuvers, exertions of the force and will the *Federalist* had assured that the judiciary lacked.

Other legal observers besides Allison took notice, at least of Judge Ludlow's aggressive intervention. A Republican lawyer in Pittsburgh read the Associated Press report of the arrest, which had chosen to give weight to Ludlow's charge to the grand jury because of "[t]he high character of Judge Ludlow as an impartial magistrate."[69] The Pittsburgh lawyer thought the claim of impartiality carried "a contradiction on its face." Otherwise, "how was it possible for" Ludlow "to have so far departed from his duty as a Judge, as to assume cognizance of a matter which was not before him, and pronounce judgment on it in advance?" In other words, the Pittsburgh lawyer had spotted Ludlow's problem and identified it as essentially the problem of the seventh impeachment article in the trial of Samuel Chase: He would act as both prosecutor and judge in such an instance. Moreover, the Pittsburgh lawyer had identified the activism of the Court of Quarter Sessions under Ludlow: The matter was not "before him," so Ludlow put it before himself.[70]

A newspaper in Philadelphia made a similar point. The *Sunday Dispatch* observed, "The intervention of Judge Ludlow of the quarter sessions, in the question, is one of the most surprising events of the week. Without any complaint being made before him on oath, with nothing but common rumor to depend upon, that Judge suddenly threw himself before the community as the voluntary accuser of the United States officers."[71] Note the language of these commentaries: "intervention," "threw himself before," "voluntary," and "pronounce judgment in advance." These Republican critics were seeking a vocabulary to describe judicial activism before such categories of thought about the judiciary in America were common parlance in the realm of political debate.

* * *

Perhaps everyone who writes on the constitutional history of the Civil War can be said to have absorbed unconsciously the lesson of *The Federalist* number 78 on the judicial branch. One able historian of the Supreme Court in the

Civil War era, for example, began his chapter on the war by stating, "Although during the Civil War, as in most major wars, the judiciary was for the most part outside the mainstream of events, the early months engaged most of the members of the depleted Supreme Court and many of the federal district judges."[72]

Without saying so explicitly, we have tacitly underwritten the assumption that the courts do not really need close historical inspection for their role in shaping the volatile political climate of the Civil War North. The reputation and profile of the Supreme Court in the Civil War have long since been recovered from the old assertion that it suffered a near fatal "self inflicted wound" in the Dred Scott decision and was in danger of mortal attack from furious Republicans in the era. Republicans in the Congress and President Lincoln himself never mounted such an attack.[73]

But that historical enterprise has caused historians consistently to ask the wrong questions about the relationships among the branches of the U.S. government under the Lincoln administration. There has been no consideration of a different view that seeks not to rescue the reputation of the court by wrapping it in political consensus but to see the judiciary as being a partisan protagonist of great force and will on important occasions. In other words, historians have been too preoccupied with what was done to the judges during the Civil War and have not thought enough about what the judges did to others.

Understanding the activist and threatening judicial context of the Civil War helps to make President Abraham Lincoln's activist view of the presidency more understandable. It is little wonder that in a cabinet meeting in September 1863 the president showed himself extremely angry—angrier than Attorney General Edward Bates, for one, had ever seen him. Lincoln was enraged at the practice of some Pennsylvania judges in discharging draftees on writs of habeas corpus. Before the cabinet, but not the public, Lincoln even threatened to banish the offending judges to the Confederacy.[74] Lincoln knew how dangerous the judiciary really was.

Notes

Introduction

1. Lerone Bennett, *Forced into Glory: Abraham Lincoln's White Dream* (Chicago: Johnson Publishing, 1999); Thomas DeLorenzo, *The Real Abraham Lincoln* (Roseville, Calif.: Prima, 2002). As of this date, customer reactions to these books number in the hundreds on Amazon.com.

2. David Herbert Donald, *Lincoln Reconsidered: Essays on the Civil War Era* (New York: Vintage, 1956), ch. 1.

Chapter 1: Lincoln and Democracy

Abraham Lincoln, *The Collected Works of Abraham Lincoln,* edited by Roy P. Basler (New Brunswick, N.J.: Rutgers University Press, 1953), 2:532 (hereafter *Collected Works*), quotes the phrase in the epigraph and then annotates it: "As I would not be a *slave,* so I would not be a *master.* This expresses my idea of democracy. Whatever differs from this, to the extent of the difference, is no democracy. A. LINCOLN—." The note reads: "The date, which has been assigned, to this document is apparently pure conjecture. The manuscript is associated with no speech or occasion known to the editors. It was given by Mrs. Lincoln to her friend Myra Bradwell of Chicago, who together with her husband, Judge James B. Bradwell, succeeded in having Mrs. Lincoln released from the institution in which she was confined as insane in her later years. The scrap of paper is unsigned, but a signature clipped from another document has been pasted below the definition." The document, which now lacks a signature but is in Lincoln's hand, is in the Illinois State Historical Library in Springfield.

1. Paul Corcoran, "The Limits of Democratic Theory," in *Democratic Theory and Practice,* edited by Graeme Duncan (New York: Cambridge University Press, 1983), ch. 2.

2. Francesca Poletta, *Freedom Is an Endless Meeting: Democracy in American Social Movements* (Chicago: University of Chicago Press, 2001).

3. *Tribune Almanac and Political Register for 1865* (New York: Tribune Association, 1865), 68. I am following Edmund S. Morgan, *Inventing the People: The Rise of Popular Sovereignty in England and the United States* (New York: W. W. Norton, 1988).

4. Gabor Boritt, ed., *Of the People, by the People, for the People* (New York: Columbia University Press, 1996). See also Benjamin Thomas, "Lincoln and Democracy," in *"Lincoln's Humor" and Other Essays,* edited by Michael Burlingame (Urbana: University of Illinois Press, 2002), 45–59. Thomas's book provides a sample of essays that merge the question of Lincoln and democracy into other issues, without direct analysis of what Lincoln meant by democracy. Most essays on Lincoln share the same fault. Roy P. Basler, *Abraham Lincoln's Democracy: An Address Delivered at Lincoln Memorial University* (Harrogate, Tenn.: Lincoln Memorial University, 1938), 2.

5. When Lincoln said "common people" he seems to have been referring not to economic caste but to the physical features of most people. Michael Burlingame, ed., *Inside Lincoln's White House: The Complete War Diary of John Hay* (Carbondale: Southern Illinois University Press, 1997), 132n343.

6. Garry Wills, *Lincoln at Gettysburg* (New York: Simon and Schuster, 1992), 129, pages 145–46 emphasize "people." Richard Nelson Current has discussed Lincoln propositions in the Gettysburg Address, suggesting that Lincoln was not interested in governing "with" the people. Richard Nelson Current, *Speaking of Abraham Lincoln: The Man and His Meaning for Our Times* (Urbana: University of Illinois Press, 1983), 56–57.

7. Mark E. Neely, *The Abraham Lincoln Encyclopedia* (New York: Da Capo Press, 1982), 261–62; James G. Randall, *Lincoln the President* (New York: Dodd-Mead, 1945), 1:380ff.

8. Jackson is quoted in Harry Watson, *Liberty and Power: The Politics of Jacksonian America* (New York: Hill and Wang, 1990), 10.

9. *Collected Works,* 1:378–79, 1:385–86.

10. The historian John Ashcroft notes that the Whig Party "maintained an almost deafening silence on the entire subject of political democracy." Watson, *Liberty and Power,* 245.

11. Stewart Winger provides a stimulating discussion of Lincoln's Whiggery in *Lincoln, Religion, and Romantic Cultural Politics* (DeKalb: Northern Illinois University Press, 2003).

12. *Collected Works,* 1:112–15.

13. Ibid., 278–79.

14. Ibid., 2:321, 4:268.

15. Don E. Fehrenbacher and Virginia Fehrenbacher, comps. and eds., *Recollected Words of Abraham Lincoln* (Stanford, Calif.: Stanford University Press, 1996), 1.

16. Thomas F. Schwartz, "'You Can Fool All of the People' Lincoln Never Said That," *For the People: A Newsletter of the Abraham Lincoln Association* 5 (Winter 2003): 1, 6, 7.

17. Truth is quoted in David Donald, *Lincoln* (New York: Scribners, 1995), 541; Frederick Douglass, *Life and Times of Frederick Douglass: His Early Life as a Slave, His Escape from Bondage, and His Complete History, Written by Himself* (New York: Collier Books, 1962), 366, 359; Burlingame, ed., *Inside Lincoln's White House,* 221.

18. Harry Jaffa, *Crisis of the House Divided: An Interpretation of the Issues in the Lincoln-Douglas Debates* (1959, repr. Chicago: University of Chicago Press, 1982), passim.

19. His declaration in a speech on the Dred Scott decision, June 26, 1857, was that equal-

ity is a "standard maxim for free society . . . constantly looked to . . . even though never perfectly attained." Lincoln liked that statement so much that he quoted it over a year later in the seventh debate with Douglas at Alton (*Collected Works,* 2:405–6, 3:301). At Gettysburg, of course, he called equality a "proposition." Paul Zall, *Abe Lincoln Laughing* (Knoxville: University of Tennessee Press, 1995); Earl Schenck Miers, ed., *Lincoln Day by Day* (Dayton: Morningside, 1991).

20. Phillip S. Paludan, "The Civil War Considered as a Crisis in Law and Order," *American Historical Review* 77 (Oct. 1972): 1013–34.

21. *Collected Works,* 6:263.

22. Mark E. Neeley Jr., *The Fate of Liberty: Abraham Lincoln and Civil Liberties* (New York: Oxford University Press, 1991).

23. *Collected Works,* 8:403.

24. *Collected Works,* 4:172.

25. Paludan, *"A People's Contest,"* 258–59.

26. *Tribune Almanac and Political Register for 1865* (New York: Tribune Association, 1865), 67–68. In 1860 Douglas (at 1,211,632 votes) and Breckenridge (277,082) combined for 1,488,714 popular votes. In 1864 McClellan received 1,797,019 votes in the free states.

27. T. J. Trowbridge, "We Are a Nation," *Atlantic Monthly* (Dec. 1864): 771.

28. *Collected Works,* 4:432, 4:429.

29. John Hay, *Inside Lincoln's White House: The Complete Civil War Diary of John Hay,* edited by Michael Burlingame and John R. Turner Ettlinger (Carbondale: Southern Illinois University Press, 1997), 208.

30. Phillip Shaw Paludan, *"The Better Angels of Our Nature": Lincoln, Propaganda and Public Opinion in the North during the Civil War* (Fort Wayne: Lincoln Museum, 1992).

31. Editorial, *Illinois Journal,* Nov. 14, 1858, 1. Lincoln's speeches, it said, "are stamped with the impress of sincerity and candor which appeals at once to the higher and nobler faculties of the mind."

32. Frederick Merk, *Manifest Destiny and Mission in American History* (New York: Vintage Books, 1963), 261–62. "A thesis that continentalist and imperialist goals were sought by the nation regardless of party or section won't do. . . . A truer expression of the national spirit was Mission. . . . It was idealistic, self denying, hopeful of divine favor for national aspirations, though not sure of it." Merk then quotes the Gettysburg Address.

33. I rely for much of this assessment on Ronald White, *Lincoln's Greatest Speech: The Second Inaugural* (New York: Simon and Schuster, 2002), 188ff.

34. Jackson is quoted in Harry Watson, *Liberty and Power: The Politics of Jacksonian America* (New York: Hill and Wang, 1990).

35. Basler argues that Lincoln's view of democracy was not "a haughty belief that we are perforce the best people under the sun" (*Lincoln's Democracy,* 6).

Chapter 2: *The Exacting Legacy of a Virtuous President*

1. Information about the editing of Lincoln's speeches can be found in Abraham Lincoln, *The Collected Works of Abraham Lincoln,* edited by Roy P. Basler (New Brunswick, N.J.: Rutgers University Press, 1953), (hereafter *Collected Works*). This note appears on page 253 of volume 4.

2. March 4, 1861, *Collected Works*, 4:262.

3. Ibid., 4:261.

4. James Buchanan said "the Confederacy is a rope of sand" in his Fourth Annual Message on December 3, 1860. The passage can be found in James Buchanan, *The Works of James Buchanan, Comprising His Speeches, State Papers, and Private Correspondence* (Philadephia: J. B. Lippincott, 1908–11), 11:12.

5. Buchanan's entire address is found in the *Works*, 11:7–43.

6. Frederic Bancroft, *The Life of William H. Seward* (New York: Harper and Brothers, 1900), 2:3.

7. "Message to Congress in Special Session," July 4, 1861, *Collected Works*, 4:430. Taney had argued in the *Merryman* case that only Congress could suspend habeas corpus and thus Lincoln had broken the law.

8. "Message to Congress in Special Session," July 4, 1861, *Collected Works*, 4:430.

9. Edward S. Corwin, *The President: Office and Powers, History and Analysis of Practice and Opinion* (New York: New York University Press, 1957), 64.

10. "To Albert Hodges," April 4, 1864, *Collected Works*, 7:281.

11. "Message to Congress in Special Session," July 4, 1861, *Collected Works*, 4:441 (annotation).

12. Edmund Wilson, *Patriotic Gore: Studies in the Literature of the American Civil War* (New York: Oxford University Press, 1966), 122.

13. Wilson, *Patriotic Gore*, 117, 120.

14. Ibid., 122.

15. Carl Becker, *The Declaration of Independence* (New York: Vintage, 1958), 216–17.

16. John G. Nicolay and John Hay, *Abraham Lincoln: A History* (New York: Century, 1893), 3:443.

17. Reinhold Niebuhr, *Leaves from the Notebook of a Tamed Cynic* (Chicago: Willett, Clark and Colby, 1929), 22.

18. John Maynard Keynes, *Essays and Sketches in Biography* (New York: Meridian Books, 1956), 266–67.

19. "Memorandum," July 3, 1861, John G. Nicolay Papers, Library of Congress.

20. *Collected Works*, 4:423.

21. "Message to Congress in Special Session," July 4, 1861, *Collected Works*, 4:441 (annotation).

22. *Collected Works*, 4:424.

23. Nicolay and Hay, *Abraham Lincoln*, 4:62–63.

24. "Message to Congress in Special Session," July 4, 1861, *Collected Works*, 4:440.

25. The ardent girlfriend of a young soldier off to war sews for him a bold banner reading "Liberty or Death!" The cautious young man prudently suggests that it be modified to "Liberty or Hurt Pretty Bad!"

26. "Message to Congress in Special Session," July 4, 1861, *Collected Works*, 4:426.

27. Don E. Fehrenbacher, *Lincoln in Text and Context: Collected Essays* (Stanford, Calif.: Stanford University Press, 1987), 121–22.

28. "To the Senate and House of Representatives," May 26, 1862, *Collected Works*, 5:241.

29. "Reply to Baltimore Committee," April 22, 1861, *Collected Works,* 4:341.

30. "To the Senate and House of Representatives," May 26, 1862, *Collected Works,* 5:242.

31. "To the Senate and House of Representatives," May 26, 1862, *Collected Works,* 5:241.

32. "To William H. Seward," June 28, 1862, *Collected Works,* 5:292.

33. "Eulogy on Henry Clay," July 6, 1852, *Collected Works,* 2:125.

34. "Message to Congress in Special Session," July 4, 1861, *Collected Works,* 4:438.

35. Phillip Paludan, *The Presidency of Abraham Lincoln* (Lawrence: University of Kansas Press, 1994), 34–35.

36. "Message to Congress in Special Session," July 4, 1861, *Collected Works,* 4:438.

37. "To Cuthbert Bullitt," July 28, 1862, *Collected Works,* 5:346.

38. "This proposal makes common cause for a common object, casting no reproaches upon any. It acts not the Pharisee. The change it contemplates would come gently as the dews of heaven, not rending or wrecking anything. Will you not embrace it?" "Proclamation Revoking General Hunter's Order of Military Emancipation of May 9, 1862," May 19, 1862, *Collected Works,* 5:223.

39. President George W. Bush to the Advisory Committee to the Lincoln Bicentennial Commission, Sept. 23, 2002.

40. "Second Inaugural Address," March 4, 1865, *Collected Works,* 8:333.

Chapter 3: Lincoln Spoils the War

1. Harry J. Carman and Reinhard H. Luthin, *Lincoln and the Patronage* (New York: Columbia University Press, 1943), 54. For a similar description of Ohio applicants in 1857—looking "awfully seedy and dingy, and others as if a scrap from the public crib would be a God's blessing"—see the altogether jaundiced Washington correspondence of the New York *Tribune,* March 24, 1857.

2. The one exception, a thorough and sound study, is that of Carman and Luthin, *Lincoln and the Patronage.* They did not have the advantage of the Abraham Lincoln MSS, not yet open to scholars, but their basic limning of the system remains unchallenged.

3. It was one not even of his own coinage. Apparently, his statement was a rephrasing of remarks about former Gov. Elbridge Gerry of Massachusetts in a biography by James T. Austin recently published. There Austin asked, "But after all, what is the worth of a victory if the enemy are allowed to possess the spoils?" Ivor Debenham Spencer, *The Victor and the Spoils: A Life of William L. Marcy* (Providence, R.I.: Brown University Press, 1959), 58–61. In Marcy's defense, he spoke rawer than he acted. As New York state comptroller he had only removed one officer—a fellow Democrat.

4. The Taylor administration is one case in point. There may have been a little under eighteen thousand federal appointments that were possible, but only 3,400 removals were made and some 2,800 resignations accepted in the first year. It was an unprecedented turnover. Holman Hamilton, *Zachary Taylor: Soldier in the White House* (New York: Bobbs-Merrill, 1951), 209. The same caution might be made of the Buchanan administration. According to the postmaster general's report late in 1858, of eight thousand postmasters appointed in the past year, 4,595 were chosen to fill vacancies due to resignation, and

only 958 to replace officers removed. The others were appointments after the incumbent postmaster had died, or, in some two thousand cases, selections to fill an entirely new office created when a post office was created. *Congressional Globe*, 35th Cong., 2d sess., appendix, 24 (Dec. 4, 1858).

5. Benjamin B. French to Henry F. French, July 3, 1853, Benjamin B. French MSS, New Hampshire Historical Society.

6. Roy F. Nichols, *The Disruption of American Democracy* (New York: Macmillan, 1948), 74–75, 82–92; Mark W. Summers, *The Plundering Generation: Corruption and the Crisis of the Union, 1849–1861* (New York: Oxford University Press, 1987), 27–28, 242–48; John Dowling to Allen W. Hamilton, March 19, 1857, Allen W. Hamilton MSS, Indiana State Library.

7. And probably for fewer than expected it. "The fees of all the consulates are overestimated," Sidney Webster wrote to a New Hampshire Democrat in 1854. "Valparaiso has been represented as very lucrative, but Gov. Wood will resign because it does not pay. [Daniel] Sickles writes here that it costs him six thousand dollars a year to live in London." A month later Webster was reporting that Nathaniel Hawthorne felt keen disappointment at his take from the Liverpool consulate, which, with the higher cost of living abroad, netted him a dead loss. Sidney Webster to John H. George, May 4, June 5, 1854, John H. George MSS, New Hampshire Historical Society.

8. Orville H. Platt to Abraham Lincoln, Aug. 11, 1862, Abraham Lincoln Presidential Papers, Library of Congress. I use the word *his* because with few exceptions nearly all the appointments went to men, and even those women chosen were often recognized as the relict or relative of a man who for various reasons (including death) could not accept the office tendered.

9. James Dixon to Abraham Lincoln, Aug. 11, 1862, Abraham Lincoln Presidential Papers, Library of Congress.

10. I am indebted for this understanding to Eric L. McKitrick, *Andrew Johnson and Reconstruction* (New York: Oxford University Press, 1960), 379–83.

11. New York *Evening Post,* April 22, 1851.

12. John A. Andrew to Abraham Lincoln, March 11, 1861, Abraham Lincoln Presidential Papers, Library of Congress.

13. *Congressional Globe,* 37th Cong., special senate session, 1497 (March 23, 1861).

14. St. Louis *Globe-Democrat,* June 6, 1884, cited in Mark Wahlgren Summers, *Party Games: Getting, Keeping, and Using Power in Gilded Age America* (Chapel Hill: University of North Carolina Press, 2004), 33.

15. On the denial that a party "against the war is just as legitimate as a party for the war," see, for example, Cincinnati *Gazette,* Feb. 18, 1863.

16. Carman and Luthin, *Lincoln and the Patronage,* 9–10.

17. Ibid., 54, citing *Diary of Adam Gurowski,* 1:16–17. In retrospect, Secretary of the Navy Gideon Welles remembered the same anomaly, of a clamor for removals "when the storm of civil war was about bursting on the country." John T. Morse in Gideon Welles, *Diary of Gideon Welles, Secretary of the Navy under Lincoln and Johnson* (Boston: Houghton-Mifflin, 1911), 1:10.

18. Carman and Luthin, *Lincoln and the Patronage,* 53, 112. For patronage dealings with Doolittle see Abraham Lincoln memorandum on Joseph G. Knapp, ca. July 15, 1861,

Abraham Lincoln, *The Collected Works of Abraham Lincoln,* edited by Roy P. Basler (New Brunswick, N.J.: Rutgers University Press, 1953), 4:449 (hereafter *Collected Works*); James Rood Doolittle to Lincoln, March 8, 1862, *Collected Works,* 5:149n; Lincoln to Doolittle, Jan. 22, 1863, *Collected Works,* 6:70.

19. *Congressional Globe,* 37th Cong., special senate session, 1497 (March 23, 1861). Trumbull later became an outspoken champion of civil service reform, but by then other Illinois Republicans were squatting in the public crib. Removals did not happen everywhere at the same speed. As late as July 1861, the *Saratogian* stormed that of sixty-one post offices in the county, Democrats had retained all but nine. In neighboring Washington County, though, the new broom had already swept clean. Albany *Atlas and Argus,* July 6, 1861.

20. Ari Hoogenboom, *Outlawing the Spoils: A History of the Civil Service Reform Movement, 1865–1883* (Urbana: University of Illinois Press, 1968), 6.

21. Providence *Post,* quoted in the Cleveland *Plain Dealer,* Oct. 28, 1862.

22. Mark Neely, *The Union Divided: Party Conflict in the Civil War North* (Cambridge, Mass.: Harvard University Press, 2002), 21–27.

23. Samuel Bowles to Henry L. Dawes, July 6, 1861, Henry Laurens Dawes MSS, Library of Congress; Oliver P. Morton to Abraham Lincoln, Aug. 20, 1862 ("fine business qualifications and one of the most influential men in the 11th Congressional District"), George C. Woodruff to Lincoln, Aug. 5, 1862, Thomas Corwin to Lincoln, March 11, 1861, and G. J. Park to Lincoln, March 4, 1861 ("a man of great legal attainments & one who is *honest* therewith"—in this case the writer insisting that none of the candidates applying from Leavenworth qualified in those respects), all in the Abraham Lincoln Presidential Papers, Library of Congress.

24. The phrase can be found regularly, but for examples see Salmon P. Chase to Abraham Lincoln, Aug. 12, 1862, Abraham Lincoln Presidential Papers, Library of Congress.

25. Hoogenboom, *Outlawing the Spoils,* 2–3.

26. Cincinnati *Daily Enquirer,* May 2, 7, 1862.

27. Cleveland *Plain Dealer,* Nov. 25, 1862.

28. Remarks of a Union colonel (and, apparently, a radical Republican), New York *Tribune,* Aug. 9, 1862.

29. Cleveland *Plain Dealer,* Nov. 12, 1862.

30. William C. Davis, *"A Government of Our Own": The Making of the Confederacy* (Baton Rouge: Louisiana State University Press, 1994), 66–67, 190–93. A few Peace Democrats argued that in this respect the Confederate constitution was superior to the document it supplanted because it struck "at the root of our corrupting patronage" and urged that the wise example be followed if the Union was restored. Letter of John L. O'Sullivan, New York *Tribune,* Aug. 1, 1862.

31. Michael F. Holt, *The Rise and Fall of the American Whig Party: Jacksonian Politics and the Onset of the Civil War* (New York: Oxford University Press, 1999), 138–39, 150, 164–65, 414–35, 549–51, 645–51, 664–71; Charles Sellers, *James K. Polk, Continentalist, 1843–1846* (Princeton: Princeton University Press, 1966), 284–99; Roy F. Nichols, *The Democratic Machine, 1850–1854* (New York: Columbia University Press, 1923), 197–220; J. B. Garvin to Horatio Seymour, March 30, 1853, and Lorenzo B. Shepard to Seymour, May 17, 1853, both in Horatio Seymour MSS, New York State Library. On Buchanan's balancing act with the offices, see David E. Meerse's endless and Argus-eyed dissertation

"James Buchanan, the Patronage, and the Northern Democratic Party, 1857–1868," Ph.D. thesis, University of Illinois, 1969. For specific bitterness at "basest treachery and most unaccountable ingratitude," see George Sanderson to William Bigler, March 24, 1857, William Bigler MSS, Historical Society of Pennsylvania; and Gideon Tucker to Edmund Burke, March 16, 1859, Edmund Burke MSS, Library of Congress.

32. Eric L. McKitrick, *Andrew Johnson and Reconstruction* (New York: Oxford University Press, 1960), 383–92; Mark Wahlgren Summers, *The Era of Good Stealings* (New York: Oxford University Press, 1993), 89–104. Michael Les Benedict points out that Johnson had some success in exacerbating rivalries between radicals and conservatives by his appointments. In Toledo, Congressman James S. Ashley's long-time antagonist A. G. Clark was chosen postmaster, and in George W. Julian's congressional district his enemy Solomon Meredith became district tax assessor. That Johnson knew what he was doing is certainly true, but whether the appointments did anything to weaken Julian or Ashley is the real question. If election results and the noise of party conventions offer any guide, Meredith and Clark found themselves pushed even further to the margins of the Republican Party. Michael Les Benedict, *A Compromise of Principle: Congressional Republicans and Reconstruction, 1863–1869* (New York: W. W. Norton, 1974), 69.

33. On deference to a member of Congress's wishes, see Salmon P. Chase to Abraham Lincoln, Aug. 4, 6, 16, 1862, Abraham Lincoln Presidential Papers, Library of Congress. On the recommendation of other Republicans as well as the member of Congress from Delaware, see Chase to Lincoln, Aug. 13, 1862, Abraham Lincoln Papers.

34. New York *Evening Post,* July 21, 1853.

35. Abraham Lincoln to Edward Bates, March 18, 1862, *Collected Works,* 5:163.

36. Thus, "If Ohio is not already overstocked with Paymasterships of Volunteers, let Richard P. L. Baber have one." Abraham Lincoln to Simon Cameron, Aug. 10, 1861, *Collected Works,* 4:480.

37. For one such case in Connecticut, see Welles, *Diary of Gideon Welles,* 1:72 (Aug. 10, 1862). Sen. James Dixon, a conservative former Know Nothing turned Republican, demanded his slate of candidates for collector and assessor under the 1862 revenue law. The governor and Republicans in the state legislature drew up a different slate, and Secretary of the Navy Gideon Welles very much wanted a candidate of his own for one of the places. When the president amended Dixon's slate to offer something to both sides, Dixon staged an aggressive letter-writing campaign and sent delegations to Washington to back up his case. Lincoln was forced to retreat. Sen. James Dixon to Frederick Seward, July 31, 1862, Dixon and Dwight Loomis to Frederick W. Seward, July 31, 1862, Dixon to Abraham Lincoln, Aug. 1, 11 (three letters), 12, 1862, Nathaniel D. Sperry to Lincoln, Aug. 6, 1862, James F. Babcock to Lincoln, Aug. 7, 1862, Orville H. Platt (state party chair) to Lincoln, Aug. 11, 1862, and Salmon Chase to Lincoln, Aug. 7, 1862, all in Abraham Lincoln Presidential Papers, Library of Congress; Abraham Lincoln to Salmon P. Chase, Aug. 14, 1862, and Lincoln to James Dixon, Aug. 21, 1862, *Collected Works,* 5:375, 5:385–86.

38. For unified slates, see Isaac N. Arnold to Abraham Lincoln, March 12, 1861, A. H. Morrison to J. M. Edmunds, Aug. 1, 1862, and Salmon P. Chase to Lincoln, Aug. 4, 6, 12, 1862, Abraham Lincoln Presidential Papers, Library of Congress.

39. As note, Abraham Lincoln to Rufus F. Andrews, Aug. 6, 1861, *Collected Works,* 4:474.

40. Abraham Lincoln to William H. Seward, Aug. 17, 1861, *Collected Works,* 4:491.

41. Abraham Lincoln to William H. Seward, Aug. 10, 1861, *Collected Works,* 4:481. Fair consideration in this case did not give the applicant the consulate he wanted.

42. Abraham Lincoln to William H. Seward, March 13, 1862, *Collected Works,* 5:158; see also Lincoln to Stanton, March 18, 1862, *Collected Works,* 5:64.

43. Abraham Lincoln to Simon Cameron, Aug. 29, 1861, *Collected Works,* 4:502.

44. Abraham Lincoln to Edwin M. Stanton, Jan. 27, 1862, *Collected Works,* 5:111.

45. Abraham Lincoln to James Pollock, Aug. 15, 1861, *Collected Works,* 4:485.

46. Abraham Lincoln to James Dixon, Aug. 21, 1862, *Collected Works,* 5:385–86.

47. For Walter Trumbull's application to the Naval Academy, see Abraham Lincoln to Gideon Welles, May 21, 1861, *Collected Works,* 4:381. For a paymastership for Sen. Jacob Collamer's son, see Abraham Lincoln to Edwin M. Stanton, Aug. 26, 1862, *Collected Works,* 5:394. For a brigade surgeon's position for Vice President Hannibal Hamlin's son, see Abraham Lincoln to Edwin M. Stanton, March 25, 1862, *Collected Works,* 5:171. For a West Point cadetship to the son of the speaker of the Pennsylvania house, see Abraham Lincoln memorandum on the appointment of David D. Johnson, ca. Jan. 6, 1864, *Collected Works,* 7:110.

48. For arguments that Lincoln was changing and beginning to tilt toward the conservatives in his appointments policy in his very last months in office, see William C. Harris, *With Charity for All: Lincoln and the Restoration of the Union* (Lexington: University Press of Kentucky, 1997), 240–41.

49. "Agate" (Whitelaw Reid), Cincinnati *Gazette,* Dec. 23, 1862.

50. Abraham Lincoln to Simon Cameron, Aug. 19, 29, 1861, *Collected Works,* 4:493, 502.

51. Summers, *The Era of Good Stealings,* 169–74, 186–95.

52. Gen. S. F. Cary, Cincinnati *Gazette,* Oct. 3, 1862.

53. On antipartyism, see Glenn C. Altschuler and Stuart M. Blumin, *Rude Republic: Americans and their Politics in the Nineteenth Century* (Princeton: Princeton University Press, 2000), 163–70.

54. Speech of Henry B. Stanton, New York *Tribune,* July 5, 1862.

55. Altschuler and Blumin, *Rude Republic,* 171–79.

56. Allan G. Bogue, *The Earnest Men: Republicans of the Civil War Senate* (Ithaca, N.Y.: Cornell University Press, 1981), 333–34.

57. For a sympathetic reading of Vallandigham, see Frank Klement, *The Limits of Dissent: Clement L. Vallandigham and the Civil War* (New York: Fordham University Press, 1998). For a much more unattractive view, and one marking the extremity of his difference from Republicans, even the most cautious, see Vallandigham's remarks, as, for example, in the *Congressional Globe,* 37th Cong. 2d sess. Ideology aside, it is my impression from the congressman's own speeches that his favorite subject remained always himself to the serious detriment of his ability to persuade or make a case against the war that required a powerful answer.

58. "E.H.L.," Cincinnati *Gazette,* Feb. 25, 1863; see also Cincinnati *Gazette,* Oct. 9, 31, Nov. 3, 1862.

59. Alvy L. King, *Louis T. Wigfall: Southern Fire-eater* (Baton Rouge: Louisiana State

University Press, 1970), 112. For Republican recollection, see Parson William G. Brownlow's Chicago speech reprinted in the Cincinnati *Gazette,* Oct. 29, 1862.

60. *Congressional Globe,* 37th Cong. 3d sess., appendix, 60 (Jan. 14, 1863), 173 (Feb. 22, 1863) or, a little more elliptically, see Clement Vallandigham's remarks on page 59: "But really, sir, if there is to be no hanging, let this Administration, and all who have done its bidding everywhere, rejoice and be exceedingly glad." The same reading might be put to the Cincinnati *Enquirer's* warning (April 19, 1862) in reference to an alleged Republican plan to "inaugurate a reign of terror": "Poisoned cups return to the lips of those who mixed them; mischief haunts the violent, and they who take up the sword perish by the sword." Let it be emphasized, however, that Republicans used bloodthirsty language of their own about enemies. The Wheeling *Intelligencer* declared it incredible that Vallandigham was allowed to live and marveled that "some Charlotte Corday, bereft of a brother, has not met him coming out of a bath, as Danton was met," or "some Orsini, bereft of a son, has not waited in a crowd for him." Of another member of Congress from New York, the reporter for the New York *Tribune* warned readers, "If he dares to open his traitorous mouth in Congress for compromise, the steps of the chamber will be *crimsoned with blood.*" See also the Cincinnati *Daily Enquirer,* April 16, 22, 1862.

61. The fortunes of the War Democrats—some within the party and some without—receives thorough treatment, at least as far as state election campaigns are concerned, in Christopher Dell, *Lincoln and the War Democrats: The Grand Erosion of Conservative Tradition* (Rutherford: Fairleigh Dickinson University Press, 1975). That book is marred, however, by the serious problem of deciding what a War Democrat was. When, for example, Dell declares (302) that Thurlow Weed was a War Democrat and supported General McClellan in 1864, the definition has become a mighty slippery thing. Weed never was a Democrat, did not support General McClellan, and did not declare against Lincoln's reelection. More troublesome, perhaps, is that Dell never goes beyond important names to examine the voting, state by state and precinct by precinct, to find how far converts could fetch and carry their old supporters.

62. Joel H. Silbey, *A Respectable Minority: The Democratic Party in the Civil War Era, 1860–1868* (New York: W. W. Norton, 1977), 140–57. On the soldier vote, see Louisville *Weekly Journal,* Oct. 4, 11, 1864; Luzerne *Union,* Dec. 7, 1864; James Buchanan to Lewis Coryell, n.d. [Sept. 1864], Lewis Coryell MSS, Historical Society of Pennsylvania; and C. M. Gould to Samuel S. Cox, Oct. 16, 1864, Samuel S. Cox MSS, Brown University.

63. McKitrick, *Andrew Johnson and Reconstruction,* 394–420. For fond hopes, see W. R. Browne to Thurlow Weed, July 2, 1866, Thurlow Weed MSS, University of Rochester. For divergent notions of what the National Union Party ought to mean, see editorials in the New York *World,* June 27, July 12, 24, 1866, and the New York *Times,* July 14, 19, 1866; see also James Dixon to Manton Marble, June 30, 1866, Fitz-John Porter to Marble, July 19, 1866, and William H. Bryant to Marble, July 25, 1866, Manton Marble MSS, Library of Congress.

64. Paul Kleppner, *The Third Electoral System, 1853–1892: Parties, Voters, and Political Cultures* (Chapel Hill: University of North Carolina Press, 1979), 74–98.

65. Summers, *The Plundering Generation.*

66. On the wartime Reconstruction in the former Confederate states see William C. Harris, *With Charity for All: Lincoln and the Restoration of the Union* (Lexington: Uni-

versity Press of Kentucky, 1997). His reading is less concerned with the governments' viability than with Lincoln's conservatism, a point open, to say the least, to great debate. For a more insightful view into the fragility of the Union parties, see Eric Foner, *Reconstruction: America's Unfinished Revolution, 1863–1877* (New York: Harper and Row, 1988), 43–45, 270–71. For the frustrations of Virginia, though, see Richard Lowe, *Republicans and Reconstruction in Virginia, 1856–70* (Charlottesville: University of Virginia Press, 1991), 16–45; and Charles H. Ambler, *Francis H. Pierpont: Union War Governor of Virginia and Father of West Virginia* (Chapel Hill: University of North Carolina Press, 1937), 220–21; see also Francis Pierpont to Waitman T. Willey, Feb. 8, March 1, 1866, Beverly Fragsen to Willey, March 27, 1866, and Charles Lewis to Willey, April 20, 1866, all in Waitman T. Willey MSS, West Virginia University Library.

67. Foner, *Reconstruction*, 37–43, 413–14, 421.

68. L. A. Sheldon to James A. Garfield, March 30, 1865, James A. Garfield MSS, Library of Congress.

69. Foner, *Reconstruction*, 182–83; Ted Tunnell, *Crucible of Reconstruction: War, Radicalism and Race in Louisiana, 1862–1877* (Baton Rouge: Louisiana State University Press, 1984), 41–50; Michael Hahn to Nathaniel P. Banks, Oct. 28, 1864, and B. Rush Plumly to Mrs. Nathaniel P. Banks, Oct. 26, 1864, Nathaniel P. Banks MSS, Library of Congress; Amos E. Simpson and Vaughn B. Baker, "Michael Hahn: Steady Patriot," *Louisiana History*, 13 (Summer 1972): 246.

70. Don A. Pardee to James A. Garfield, July 15, 1866, James A. Garfield MSS, Library of Congress.

71. On the legislature's makeup and purposes, see E. Hiestand to Nathaniel P. Banks, Nov. 19, 1865, Nathaniel P. Banks MSS, Library of Congress; and L. A. Sheldon to James A. Garfield, Dec. 16, 1865, James A. Garfield MSS, Library of Congress.

72. As L. A. Sheldon noted in his letter to Garfield (Dec. 16, 1865): "When he wants to conciliate the rebels he appoints them to office, but when they attempt to interfere with his selfish plans, he lifts over their head the military cudgel and reminds them of the strong hand at Washington which he can command."

73. Foner, *Reconstruction*, 197, 262–63; Tunnell, *Crucible of Reconstruction*, 95–107.

Chapter 4: *"Seeking a Cause of Difficulty with the Government"*

The material in this chapter formed part of a lecture delivered on October 7, 2004, at the University of Illinois at Springfield. Much revised and expanded nearly threefold since that time, this portion of the lecture has benefited greatly from an astute reading with copious commentary by Herman Belz of the University of Maryland; from very helpful comments by Phillip S. Paludan, who heard the lecture in its original form and read the revised versions based on it; and from much information, insight, and criticism supplied in correspondence and conversations with Jonathan White, a graduate student in history at the University of Maryland. William Blair, my colleague and director of the George and Ann Richards Civil War Era Center at Penn State, also patiently read the last version and offered advice and criticism.

1. James Madison, Alexander Hamilton, and John Jay, *The Federalist*, edited by Clinton Rossiter (1961, repr. New York: New American Library, 1999), 433.

2. See especially Don E. Fehrenbacher, "Roger B. Taney and the Sectional Crisis," *Journal of Southern History* 43 (Nov. 1977): 555–66.

3. The aggressively sectional and political nature of the decision is the point of Don E. Fehrenbacher, *The Dred Scott Case: Its Significance in American Law and Politics* (New York: Oxford University Press, 1978).

4. *The War of the Rebellion: A Compilation of the Official Records of the Union and Confederate Armies*, 128 vols. (Washington: Government Printing Office, 1880–1902), ser. 2, vol. 1, pp. 574–76. For an assessment of Merryman's actions more severe than that, see James M. McPherson, *Battle Cry of Freedom: The Civil War Era* (New York: Oxford University Press, 1988), 287–88. Merryman's description of the arrest can be found in the entry on "Habeas Corpus" in *The American Annual Cyclopaedia and Register of Important Events of the Year 1861* (New York: D. Appleton, 1862), 354.

5. Carl B. Swisher, *The Oliver Wendell Homes Devise History of the Supreme Court of the United States*, vol. 5: *The Taney Period, 1836–1864* (New York: Macmillan, 1974), 846–50. See also *American Annual Cyclopaedia*, 355–56.

6. Swisher, *The Oliver Wendell Homes Devise History of the Supreme Court of the United States*, 5:846–47. At the time, Supreme Court justices also served as federal court justices on an assigned circuit, and Baltimore was on Taney's circuit. Swisher also points out that the circuit court judge who would ordinarily have sat with Taney to form the circuit court bench there, William F. Giles, stayed away when Taney issued the decision in the Merryman case. Giles had already issued a writ of habeas corpus three weeks earlier seeking the release of a minor who enlisted in the Union Army against his parents' consent. War afforded the judiciary many opportunities to intervene in national affairs, and those in Maryland were not shy about doing so. Mark E. Neely Jr., *The Fate of Liberty: Abraham Lincoln and Civil Liberties* (New York: Oxford University Press, 1991), 9.

7. Alfred H. Kelly, Winfred A. Harbison, and Herman Belz, *The American Constitution: Its Origins and Development, Volume 1*, seventh ed. (New York: W. W. Norton, 1991), 304; *Ex parte Merryman* at http//web.lexis-nexis.com, page 1, accessed Sept. 28, 2004. Confusion reigned at the time, even among those who reprinted the decision. Thus the *American Law Register* (9 [July 1861]: 524) headed the case as "In the United States Circuit Court, Chambers, Baltimore, Md. before Taney, Chief Justice."

8. That is the way, more or less, Don E. Fehrenbacher put it in *Slavery, Law, and Politics: The Dred Scott Case in Historical Perspective* (New York: Oxford University Press, 1981), 183.

9. *Ex parte Merryman*, http://web.lexis-nexis.com, page 7, accessed Sept. 28, 2004.

10. Swisher, *The Oliver Wendell Homes Devise History of the Supreme Court of the United States*, 5:846.

11. Ibid., 308.

12. Ibid., 316.

13. Ibid., 317.

14. McPherson, *Battle Cry of Freedom*, 266.

15. Swisher, *The Oliver Wendell Homes Devise History of the Supreme Court of the United States*, 5:850. See, for example, *The Opinion of the Hon. Roger Brooke Taney, in the Habeas Corpus Case of John Merryman* (Baltimore: Lucas Brothers, 1861), and *Decision of Chief Justice Taney in the Merryman Case . . .* (Philadelphia: John Campbell, 1862). The decision apparently appeared first in the Baltimore *American* newspaper on June 3, 1861.

16. Stanley I. Kutler, *Judicial Power and Reconstruction Politics* (Chicago: University of Chicago Press, 1968), ch. 1.

17. Harold M. Hyman, *A More Perfect Union: The Impact of the Civil War and Reconstruction on the Constitution* (New York: Alfred A. Knopf, 1973), 256.

18. The most extended treatment and defense of the institution can be found in Ralph Lerner, "The Supreme Court as Republican Schoolmaster," *The Supreme Court Review 1967,* edited by Philip B. Kurland (Chicago: University of Chicago Press, 1967), esp. 127–55.

19. William Rehnquist attributes the loose nature of the charges to the grand jury made by the early federal judiciary to the scantiness of federal laws to enforce and to the habit of filling the time customarily allotted to the charge anyway. Rehnquist, *Grand Inquests: The Historic Impeachments of Justice Samuel Chase and President Andrew Johnson* (New York: William Morrow, 1992), 95. Ralph Lerner distinguished the "abuse" of the charge from its legitimate educational function in part by the fact that later Federalists like Samuel Chase employed the charge to criticize the law they were sworn to uphold. Lerner, "The Supreme Court as Republican Schoolmaster," 135. Otherwise Lerner identified abuse only by degree and tone of the charge.

20. Quoted in Rehnquist, *Grand Inquests,* 94. The Baltimore charge was what brought President Jefferson to suggest Chase's impeachment. Kelly, Harbison, and Belz, *The American Constitution,* 168; Keith Whittington, *Constitutional Construction: Divided Powers and Constitutional Meaning* (Cambridge: Harvard University Press, 1999), 22.

21. Rehnquist, *Grand Inquests,* 90–91.

22. Ibid., 104; Whittington, *Constitutional Construction,* 38.

23. Rehnquist, *Grand Inquests,* 93.

24. Kelly, Harbison, and Belz, *The American Constitution,* 169.

25. Swisher, *The Oliver Wendell Homes Devise History of the Supreme Court of the United States,* 5:858–61.

26. For a view of the Taney court's activism see Fehrenbacher, *The Dred Scott Case,* 232. On the charge to the grand jury see Richard D. Younger, *The People's Panel: The Grand Jury in the United States, 1634–1941* (Providence: Brown University Press, 1963), 106–8, 133.

27. See, for example, the charge to the U.S. Circuit Court grand jury by Supreme Court Justice Samuel F. Miller in June 1863. Dubuque *Herald,* June 3, 1863.

28. Lerner, "The Supreme Court as Republican Schoolmaster," 131.

29. For a glimpse inside a grand jury in the era see *A Philadelphia Perspective: The Diary of Sidney George Fisher,* edited by Nicholas Wainwright (Philadelphia: Historical Society of Pennsylvania, 1967), 333, 335–36, 338–39.

30. Lerner, "The Supreme Court as Republican Schoolmaster," 132.

31. Younger, *The People's Panel,* 108 and note.

32. Allan Nevins, *Ordeal of the Union: A House Dividing, 1852–1857* (New York: Charles Scribner's Sons, 1947), 434–35. Controversy surrounds Lecompte's role. Nevins, following press reports for the 1850s, says the justice made accusations of "constructive treason," a legal doctrine made obsolete by John Marshall in the Aaron Burr conspiracy case a half century earlier. James C. Malin offers a labored but more precise defense of Lecompte's competence in "Judge Lecompte and the 'Sack of Lawrence,' May 21, 1856," *Kansas Historical Quarterly,* 20 (Aug. 1953): 464–94, esp. 473. The Chicago *Tribune,* citing a St. Louis source, reported the charge to the grand jury for "high treason" on May 13, 1856. See also Chicago *Tribune,* May 18, May 20, May 22, Aug. 16, 1856.

33. Democratic critics of the arrest rightfully pointed out that the timing and removal of the victim were obviously calculated to avoid local courts, which, of course, were not open at night.

34. Philadelphia *Public Ledger,* Jan. 31, 1863. The case was described under "Habeas Corpus," *American Annual Cyclopaedia and Register of Important Events of the Year 1863* (New York: D. Appleton, 1864), 470–72, although no writ of habeas corpus was requested or issued. A modern historian of the institution of the grand jury depicts the case as an instance of the grand jury rising to the challenge to civil liberty and ignores the role of Judge Ludlow. "News of the incident prompted grand jurors attending the Philadelphia Court of Quarter Sessions to drop all other business and investigate the affair," he writes. Younger, *The People's Panel,* 111.

35. *American Annual Cyclopaedia,* 470–71.

36. James Dunlop, ed., *The General Laws of Pennsylvania, from the Year 1700, to April 22, 1846* . . . (Philadelphia: J. W. Johnson, 1847), 881, 882, 888; *Laws of the General Assembly of the State of Pennsylvania* . . . *1843* (Harrisburg: 1843), 63; *Laws of Pennsylvania* . . . *1843* (Harrisburg: 1843), 8; *Laws of Pennsylvania* . . . *1848* (Harrisburg: 1848), 25; *Laws of Pennsylvania* . . . *1851* (Harrisburg: 1851), 648, 650. See also Philadelphia *Public Ledger,* Oct. 10, 1857, Oct. 2, 1861. The judges ran on party tickets and were opposed by candidates for the other party.

37. Thus one historian has minimized *Ex parte Merryman* as "Chief Justice Taney's solo performance." Kutler, *Judicial Power and Reconstruction Politics,* 52.

38. Philadelphia *Inquirer,* Jan. 24, 1863 (under "Legal Intelligence").

39. Ezra J. Warner, *Generals in Blue: Lives of the Union Commanders* (Baton Rouge: Louisiana State University Press, 1964), 423.

40. Robert S. Harper, *Lincoln and the Press* (New York: McGraw-Hill, 1951), 233–35.

41. Indeed, one Republican newspaper regarded the grand jury's statement as a rebuke to the eager judge. Harrisburg *Telegraph,* Jan. 31, 1863.

42. Harper, *Lincoln and the Press,* 235.

43. Younger, *The People's Panel,* 64.

44. *Commonwealth v. Krubeck,* 23 Pa. C.C. 35, 1899 WL 4990 (Pa. Quar. Sess.): 1–2. http://campus.westlaw.com/result/dctopnavigation.aspx?cnt=DOC&cxt=DC&rs=WL W5.0 . . , accessed on March 25, 2005.

45. Philadelphia *Public Ledger,* Feb. 3, 1863.

46. Ibid.

47. Ibid.

48. Ibid.

49. In addition to the Pennsylvania newspapers cited in notes to follow, I examined the McKean County *Democrat,* the Pittsburgh *Gazette Times* and *Daily Dispatch,* and the Bellefonte *Central Press.* Of those four, only the McKean County newspaper was Democratic.

50. Harrisburg *Telegraph,* Jan. 29, 1863.

51. Washington (Pa.) *Reporter and Tribune,* Feb. 11, 1863. The newspaper was apparently following the lead and benefiting from the research of John Forney's Philadelphia *Press,* which originally made the comparison with the patriots of 1777. The Democratic Harrisburg *Patriot and Union* dismissed the argument by pointing out that there was no constitution in 1777 (Jan. 31, 1863, issue, answering Forney).

52. Harrisburg *Patriot and Union,* Jan. 31, 1863.

53. Harrisburg *Patriot and Union,* Feb. 2, 1863. The Democratic Pittsburgh *Post* praised "Judge Ludlow's decree" and surmised that the attempts to silence Boileau must have been the work of Republican editor John W. Forney, who had apparently been roundly criticized in Boileau's *Evening Journal* in the past.

54. York (Pa.) *Gazette,* Feb. 10, 1863.

55. Bellefonte (Pa.) *Democratic Watchman,* Feb. 6, 1863.

56. On the point in general see Mark E. Neely Jr., *The Union Divided: Party Conflict in the Civil War North* (Cambridge, Mass.: Harvard University Press, 2002), 89–117.

57. Philadelphia *Public Ledger,* Feb. 3, 1863.

58. Philadelphia *Public Ledger,* Feb. 2, 1863.

59. The Harrisburg *Patriot and Union* and the Pittsburgh *Post,* Democratic newspapers, quoted the *World* at length on February 2, 1863.

60. Samuel S. Cox, *Eight Years in Congress, from 1857–1865. Memoir and Speeches* (New York: D. Appleton, 1865), 288.

61. The Bill of Rights appeared in the Pittsburgh *Post* on February 4, 1863; "Malicious Mischief" appeared in the issue of February 6.

62. New York *Tribune,* Feb. 2, 1863. For a view that freedom of speech and press developed earlier, see Leonard Levy, *Jefferson and Civil Liberties: The Darker Side* (1963, repr. Chicago: Ivan R. Dee, 1989), 50–55.

63. New York *Times,* Feb. 4, 1863.

64. New York *Herald,* Jan. 31, 1863.

65. New York *Herald,* Feb. 3, 1863.

66. By a law of 1848 the Court of Quarter Sessions was to hold a new session on the first Monday in April, June, October, December, and February. *Laws of Pennsylvania . . . 1848,* 25.

67. Philadelphia *Public Ledger,* Feb. 3, 1863.

68. Harrisburg *Telegraph,* Feb. 3, 1863.

69. New York *Tribune,* Jan. 30, 1863.

70. Pittsburgh *Gazette-Times,* Jan. 31, 1863.

71. Quoted in the Harrisburg *Telegraph,* Feb. 2, 1863.

72. Swisher, *The Oliver Wendell Homes Devise History of the Supreme Court of the United States,* 5:841.

73. Kutler, *Judicial Power and Reconstruction Politics,* vii, revised the "self inflicted wound" argument. For the old but persistent view of the court's inherent passivity in wartime see Carl B. Swisher: "[I]n this time of civil war the strident and clamourous voice of Mars too often drowned out the voice of the law, with its stress upon reason and rightness rather than upon ruthless power, and little deference was accorded to judicial spokesmen. To a considerable degree the executive won dominance in matters which in other times would have been left to the courts." Swisher, *The Oliver Wendell Homes Devise History of the Supreme Court of the United States,* 5:974.

74. On the cabinet meeting see *The Salmon P. Chase Papers,* vol. 1: *Journals, 1829–1872,* edited by John Niven (Kent, Ohio: Kent State University Press, 1993), 441–44, and *The Diary of Edward Bates, 1859–1866,* edited by Howard K. Beale (Washington: Government Printing Office, 1933), 306–7.

Contributors

PHILLIP SHAW PALUDAN is the Naomi B. Lynn Distinguished Chair of Lincoln Studies at the University of Illinois at Springfield. He is the winner of the Bardoness Lincoln Award and the Lincoln Prize and author of *Victims: A True Story of the Civil War, The Presidency of Abraham Lincoln,* and other volumes.

WILLIAM LEE MILLER, professor of religious studies emeritus at the University of Virginia, is the author of *Lincoln's Virtues.*

MARK W. SUMMERS is a professor of history at the University of Kentucky. Among his books are *The Plundering Generation: Corruption and the Crisis of the Union, 1848–1861, The Era of Good Stealings,* and *The Gilded Age: Or the Hazard of New Functions.*

MARK E. NEELY JR., professor of history at Pennsylvania State University, won a Pulitzer Prize for *The Fate of Liberty: Abraham Lincoln and Civil Liberties* and is the author of many other volumes and articles on Lincoln.

Index

The University of Illinois Press
is a founding member of the
Association of American University Presses.

———————————————————

Composed in 10.5/13 Adobe Minion Pro
by Jim Proefrock
at the University of Illinois Press
Manufactured by Thomson-Shore, Inc.

University of Illinois Press
1325 South Oak Street
Champaign, IL 61820-6903
www.press.uillinois.edu